Contents

2110

Educational Gymnastics

Step by step

Acknowledgements

The photographs were taken by Andrew Long and Geoff Roberts.

The staff and pupils of the following schools are thanked for their unstinting co-operation:

St. Mary's C. of E. Primary School, Bridgwater

Bishop Henderson C. of E. Primary School, Taunton

Archbishop Cranmer C. of E. Primary School, Taunton

Priorswood Secondary School, Taunton.

British Library Cataloguing in Publication Data

Long, Bruce
 Educational Gymnastics
 1. Gymnastics–Study and teaching
 1. Title
 796 4'1   GV461
 ISBN 0 7131 0623 9 ✓

First published 1982
Impression number 17 16 15 14 13 12 11 10 9 8
Year   1999 1998 1997 1996 1995 1994

Printed in Great Britain for Hodder & Stoughton Educational, a division of Hodder Headline Plc, 338 Euston Road, London NW1 3BH by The Bath Press, Avon.

Introduction

Gymnastics can be taught in two different ways. In formal gymnastics children are taught predetermined specific gymnastic movements, e.g. forward rolls, backward rolls, headsprings. Children know exactly what is expected of them and therefore they and their teachers can gauge very accurately how well these activities have been performed because the various gymnastic movements are described and illustrated in many textbooks. Children conform to exact movements and standards as set for them by their teachers. Formal gymnastics is typifed by the various B.A.G.A. activities and is extremely popular and valuable for many children. Most teachers agree, however, that this approach should normally be used only in school gymnastic clubs.

The second approach to the teaching of gymnastics and that which is covered in this book is normally recommended for use during physical education lessons. In educational gymnastics children are set action tasks which are concerned with natural activities such as running, jumping, twisting, turning, hanging, rolling and spinning, balancing, transferring weight from one part or set of parts to another. They may also be set quality tasks which are concerned with how these activities are performed, e.g. at high level or low level, quickly, slowly, with acceleration, heavily, lightly.

The tasks chosen for any one lesson follow a common theme and most teachers develop this theme over five or six lessons before continuing on to the next theme. The

work is carried out on the floor for the first part of the lesson and then on suitable apparatus for the remainder of the lesson. Other forms of physical education, such as games skills, are not included in gymnastic lessons because they would not conform to the overall theme of the lesson.

Some tasks, used especially when a new idea is being introduced, can be answered in many ways, e.g. 'find many parts of your body on which you can balance'. Some tasks, usually set when an idea has been well understood and the children have become more skilful, can be answered in fewer ways, e.g. 'find some good but difficult balances on your shoulders'.

Children are normally expected to experiment in order to find the best answer to the given task. Older children are then expected to practise and improve this answer for very high quality work. There will be occasions when children will develop their work as they are performing it. However, the more experienced children become, the more they should be expected to plan their answer to a particular task before performing it.

While the children are practising their answers to the tasks set, the teacher helps them by coaching individually, or in groups, or as a class. Group or class coaching has to be couched in general terms like 'make sure that no one can hear you when you land', or 'stretch further and further till you can go no further', so that what is said applies to all. Individual coaching, however, can be far more explicit. Normally the teacher first discovers exactly what it is that the child is trying to achieve and then helps him to do so most successfully. Sometimes, especially when the teacher is more experienced, she will make alternative suggestions like 'what about balancing on your toes instead of your knees?' or 'I think your sequence would flow better if you turned in mid air'. She must be careful not to impose her ideas too strongly on the child but instead to help him to develop his own ideas and actions.

As stated previously, tasks fall into two categories:
(i) Action tasks (concentrating on natural activities). Because gymnastics is all about activity, teachers will most frequently concentrate on action tasks, especially with younger children. They will require their children to experience a full range of movements/activities but at the same time will encourage them to perform them skilfully and in various ways.
(ii) Quality tasks (concentrating on how the activities are performed). There will be times, particularly with older children, when teachers consider it important that the class's attention be focused more on quality tasks than action tasks. To take an example, children might be told that the lesson is primarily concerned with speed (how much time is used and how it is used in performing an action). They could then perform a variety of activities very quickly, very slowly, with acceleration, with deceleration and at a whole range of speeds somewhere in between. They would learn among other things that the speed at which an activity is performed can totally alter its character, that an activity may be best performed at a certain speed, and that this probably differs with each person.

These movement qualities can be placed into four categories:
(i) Time – how much time is used in or during the

performance of an activity and the way in which it is used. Depending on the time factor, actions can be quick, slow, sudden (staccato), sustained (prolonged), accelerating, decelerating and rhythmical.

(ii) Space - how children use their own bubble of space, and also how they use the shared space of the hall in relation to each other, the apparatus and the floor. Consideration must be given to whether children work near the floor or far from it (level); whether they travel forwards, backwards or sideways (direction); in direct, indirect, straight or curving lines (pathways); towards, away from, around each other or apparatus (relationships).

(iii) Flow - the degree and type of continuity on a movement. A person can decide to perform an activity in such a way that either it can be stopped easily at any time, or it cannot be arrested at will at any time during its performance except at the end. Most primary school gymnastics fall somewhere between these extremes; verve and attack will often be involved but work should also be under reasonable control. Children should be given the chance to work vigorously, even if not with absolute abandon.

(iv) Weight - the degree of muscular effort and tension used in the performance of an action. It can range from heavy and strong to light; the weight used will depend on the intention of the gymnast. Although infrequently used as a source of gymnastic tasks for young children, it is a quality which a teacher should be able to discern in her children's activity in order that she can help them improve.

Given good teaching and planning, the educational gymnastics approach has many advantages. Children certainly enjoy it thoroughly because the work takes into account their own wishes and body type, and it also allows them to be inventive and successful in their own right and at their own level. It must be admitted, however, that this approach has to be planned and taught extremely well because otherwise children will soon become bored with repetitive, low-level and undemanding activities. Children require to be worked hard physically and mentally as well as in exciting ways. They also enjoy making progress and doing things well and therefore expect teachers to help them to do this.

Progress will take place most easily within individual classes and even more so throughout the school if the themes are taught in an order followed by all teachers. Obviously things do not always go according to plan - thank goodness - and it is important to learn from and react to unexpected developments, strengths and weaknesses, moods and wishes as and when they arise. If the work that children produce is very good but different from that which was expected and intended, then good teachers will often adapt or depart from their original plan. However, this teaching on the spur of the moment should take place against the background of a commonly accepted scheme of work and the general agreement that, when substantial departures from it take place, details will be given to the teacher who takes that particular class the following year.

No two people will ever arrive at exactly the same ideal order in which to teach themes, but all will agree that some themes are applicable to certain age and/or experience groups. To take just one example, that of balancing, we all know that five-year-olds can balance quite well on their feet when stationary or when walking; to ask them to balance on their hands, to balance on a high piece of apparatus, to balance on someone else, to counterbalance with someone else or to balance on a piece of moving apparatus would be quite inappropriate and potentially dangerous. However,

children do become capable of performing these activities in a fairly predictable order and therefore these tasks should be set when the children have a very good chance of performing them successfully and skilfully. The same applies to all the other themes which teachers use. A school scheme of work can be formulated, but teachers must be free sometimes to depart from it.

How to use the book

The theme order given in this book has been found suitable for many schools and so it is suggested that it be followed for the first year or two at least. Experience in an individual school might suggest that alterations be made to it in ensuing years. Classes should be allocated certain themes according to their age and this will pose no difficulties for the younger children. Older children, however, would experience difficulty if they were taught the more advanced themes without having had experience of the easier ones. In this case, the teacher should cover the earlier themes fairly quickly before getting on to the themes allocated to her class. Certainly, as with other subjects, it is never wise to teach advanced subject matter to children who have not covered the basic material. In any case the position should be righted in the second year.

The material given on each theme is sufficient for about six lessons. Six columns, one for each lesson, have been provided opposite the suggested activities. Preparation and a record of each lesson's work can easily be made by inserting a tick or order number in the appropriate column. The activities on a page are not necessarily in the best order, (this will be dictated by the class's reaction) and it is not essential that all are taught. Spaces have been left for teachers to include additional activities of their own choice which flow from the work produced by the children or from their own experience.

There might well be occasions, especially with younger children, when teachers will deem it best to spend only two or three lessons on a particular theme before passing on to the next one. They will probably return to the original theme at a later date and continue from where they had left off. (The marks in the columns will remind them of what they had previously taught.) Generally, the standard of work and the imagination shown by the children will be enhanced the second time round because they can bring more experience to bear when responding to the tasks set by the teacher.

In the main, adult terms have been used in this book because language is very individual to the teacher and class.

Support themes

A normal way of enriching the children's work is to devote several lessons to a given theme and then to introduce a support theme to run alongside it. The gymnasts would now need to bear in mind two ideas while planning and executing their work. The main theme might be an action task like 'move on feet only' or 'balance on two parts, then overbalance into a roll and travel into another balance'. A support theme might then be added to enrich the work, e.g. 'introduce a change of speed', 'introduce a change of direction', 'follow an indirect pathway', 'sometimes work symmetrically and sometimes asymmetrically'. To help teachers to enrich their work in this way, suitable support themes have been suggested in each theme.

Most lessons will have the following structure:
(i) An opening activity. On entering the hall the children normally start work straight away; stragglers should not prevent the others from working. In order to prepare their bodies for the more vigorous work of the main part of the lesson, large movements and travelling using the whole space of the hall should be encouraged. The teacher might ask the class to choose a movement from a previous lesson, to practise a favourite movement or one which they find difficult, or she might set a simple task which the children can get on with straight away.

Gymnastic movements often demand the ability to take weight on the hands and the ability to roll; the opening activity and the closing activity present regular opportunities for these experiences.
(ii) Floorwork. The main theme is then taught on the floor. The proportion of the lesson devoted to floorwork will depend on the complexity of the theme and whether or not it is new to the children, but usually floorwork takes up just less than half of the time available for the gymnastic lesson. Two or three floorwork tasks usually provide sufficient material for one lesson. Individual tasks are sometimes repeated in several lessons.

Very occasionally, a gymnastic lesson might consist solely of either floor or apparatus work, but the normal procedure is for both aspects to be included so that the lessons learned on the floor can be applied immediately to the apparatus.
(iii) Apparatus work. Children always look forward to this part of the lesson because they find it exciting and stimulating - so much so that teachers have to remind them frequently to use the floor and the space around the apparatus as well as the apparatus itself. In most cases one apparatus task will provide enough material for each lesson. Because this part of the lesson allows children to practise on the apparatus what they have learned on the floor, because they are eager to do so, and because their memory fades over a day or so, it is important that most lessons contain floorwork and apparatus work. This means that the apparatus has to be erected and removed each lesson otherwise there is not enough room for good vigorous floorwork. However, given good procedures and training, children are capable of getting apparatus out in well under two minutes, and as a by-product, they learn safe lifting and carrying procedures and social skills concerned with working together.
(iv) A closing activity. In normal circumstances, when the children have put away their own piece of apparatus, they should assist other groups with their apparatus and then work individually answering a given task in a space on the floor. In this way the class is brought back together as a unit before leaving the hall to return to the classroom. The teacher will usually comment constructively on how the class has worked, giving praise whenever possible, while the children are changing back into their normal clothes.

Teaching methods and practices

Use of apparatus
The general rule-of-thumb is that children should only work on apparatus that they are capable of carrying safely by themselves or with others. In this way, small children will lift and use pieces of apparatus like mats, benches, skittles, canes, ropes. They will be taught exactly how to handle them, for example, they will learn to carry canes vertically, holding them near the top; infants will lift, carry and lower

(not drop) mats by holding a corner each; mats must not be placed too near radiators, walls or other mats; benches must be carried with at least one person at each end. Children will be given plenty of practice and will soon be able to get apparatus in and out very quickly as well as work on it with confidence.

One aim in apparatus work, as in floorwork, is to keep the children working all the time - no waiting for their turn. This will mean having many small teams and giving each team its own simple piece of apparatus on which to work. When children learn to approach their piece of apparatus from many directions and to use the floor as well as the apparatus, all queues will disappear.

Gradually over the years, they will learn to handle and work on larger pieces or groupings of linked apparatus, but because this will be done against the background of experience, they will be able to handle and use it with speed, efficiency and confidence. In addition, because children are progressing on to more demanding apparatus, they do not become bored. Rather, the more advanced apparatus is an exciting prospect for the future.

Apparatus should be selected and sited not only to suit the strength and experience of the children in the class, but also to suit the theme being taught. To take a couple of examples, the apparatus which will assist gymnasts to work at various levels will be very different from that used in a theme concerned with following a variety of indirect and direct horizontal pathways. It is clear therefore that apparatus should not be left out for several classes to use. Teachers ought not to arrange for older boys to erect the apparatus before the lesson, nor should they devote alternate lessons to floorwork and apparatus work. Rather, the handling of apparatus should be regarded as an important learning process in its own right; it should be seen as an opportunity for teaching safe lifting and lowering techniques and for teaching children to work with others.

The following practices should enable children to get out apparatus in a rehearsed and efficient but unhurried way:

1 The same apparatus layout, with minor variations, should normally be used for all the lessons on a given theme with children handling the same piece of apparatus every time.
2 The children should be taught the specific skills of handling each piece of apparatus.
3 Apparatus should be lifted and lowered, never dragged or dropped.
4 Children should handle apparatus with care and deliberation but no haste.
5 All large pieces of apparatus require at least two children to move or assemble them.
6 All long pieces of apparatus, however light, should be carried by at least two children, one at each end.
7 Children should normally face each other when carrying apparatus.
8 Landing mats should be provided where children are required to land from a considerable height.
9 Apparatus should normally be at least two metres away from a wall or an unrelated piece of apparatus.
10 Children should be trained to check for themselves that the apparatus is correctly assembled, but the teacher should always oversee the preparations and inspect large or complicated pieces of apparatus herself.
11 Children using small, simple apparatus should be told to start work as soon as they have checked that their apparatus is safely assembled (one pupil should be

appointed as leader). Teams using large or complicated apparatus should await the teacher's approval before starting work.

12 The teacher should normally be positioned where she can see the whole class and this will usually mean her operating from the edges of the hall and looking inwards.

13 Children should be trained to obey the word 'stop'.

14 It pays to have the apparatus stored against or fixed to the walls close to where it is likely to be used. If mats have to be stored on top of each other in one place, they need to be moved in an orderly fashion; more haste, less speed and damage. They take up less space if stored vertically against a wall.

Teachers have to decide whether a group of children is to be allocated to a certain grouping of apparatus and is to be rotated every few minutes, or if each child is to move freely from one grouping of apparatus to another. There are certainly advantages and disadvantages in both methods, but the first mentioned is more often used for junior children in order to encourage them to repeat and improve their activities. Free movement to and from apparatus is sometimes used for infants who need to experiment quite freely and at their own volition. It can also be used with great advantage with mature and experienced gymnasts who can produce sequences which involve travelling on and between several groupings of apparatus. When using this method, it is difficult to ensure that each child uses all the apparatus. There should not normally be more than five children in a team and they should practise on several pieces of apparatus each lesson. For the ensuing lesson children should start work on the next piece of apparatus; they become frustrated if they always start on their 'home' apparatus and never work on pieces of apparatus towards the end of their circuit.

The order of rotation should also prevent the possibility of body strain. For example, if a team has used a piece of apparatus which involves hanging from the arms, they should move to apparatus requiring the use of other muscles.

Partner and group work
Children love to work together in small groups but must be educated to do so efficiently and well by working in the early stages in twos without physical contact and by having their attention drawn to the need for co-operation. Activities involving co-operative contact and competition will be introduced with older children. The emphasis must then be on competing against each other in a friendly but serious way; the result of any competition is important, but not so important that children might be tempted to take advantage of each other and cheat. The co-operative work can develop to involve groups of four or five working together to produce high quality combined work. A certain amount of discussion is essential and desirable, but it must be purposeful and be kept to a minimum.

Links between educational gymnastics and formal gymnastics
The points of contact between these two forms of gymnastics are numerous and it is important for each school to decide its policy. Are both types to be kept entirely separate - educational gymnastics during lesson time and formal gymnastics during club time?

What happens if, in answer to an educational gymnastic task set by a teacher, a child performs an activity which with minor alterations could become a known agility or vault, e.g. handspring, handstand, headstand? Obviously the teacher first helps the child to improve his or her own movement. Soon, however, she has to decide whether or not to suggest that the child alters his movement slightly and so learns a formal gymnastic activity. On the one hand there is a danger that the child and teacher might become stereotyped in their thinking and come to believe that formal gymnastic movements are preferable to those 'invented' by the child. On the other hand, without help a child might not experience what could be a very exciting and rewarding activity unless he joins the gymnastic club. If the teacher does decide to coach the child to perform the new activity, she must ensure that no undue importance is attached to it because the child might subsequently perform it too frequently. Even more importantly, she must be capable of teaching that movement safely and of providing support for it if necessary.

Links between educational gymnastics and other physical activities
Most schools are able to offer many of the following activities either as part of normal lesson times or during lunch time and evening sessions: educational gymnastics, sports gymnastics, games, dancing, swimming and maybe outdoor pursuits. Because educational gymnastics is largely concerned with natural activities, it follows that what is learned in those lessons can be applied in some measure to the other physical activities. For example, the gymnastic skills of jumping and landing, flight, changing speed, changing direction, changing pathways, the use of space, twisting and turning, partner work as well as many

others are used extensively in most games. Many gymnastic skills are also used in everyday life; lifting, carrying, pulling and pushing are obvious examples, but posture, effort, ability to work at heights and the many other ways in which children learn to manage their bodies skilfully in gymnastics will also serve them well in everyday life as children and when they become adults.

It is important that children are at least made aware of these uses. If, for example, children are being taught to run, jump, reach in mid-air, land and either change direction on landing or land under complete control to stop, it would seem a pity if they were not at least told that these skills will be used in soccer, netball, skittleball, etc.

The question should be asked, 'Ought we specifically to teach these "other" skills during gymnastic lessons?' The vast majority of primary school teachers believe in cross fertilisation between the various subject areas - all they disagree upon is how this should be carried out. Some believe that the 'other' physical education skills should be taught separately but at about the same time. I believe that, where applicable, a few minutes of the gymnastic lesson should be spent on showing how the theme being taught could be applied in non-gymnastic ways. To take two examples, if I were helping children to learn how to change direction, I might well draw their attention to how the skills being learned could be applied to soccer, skittle-ball, netball, etc., or, if they were learning how to jump high into the air, I might show how this skill could be used when receiving a pass in a game of netball or when jumping to head a football.

The cardinal point to remember is that the 'other' skills should flow out of the gymnastic theme being covered and should not be the reason for it. In other words, heading a football, for example, should be taught specifically in a games lesson and the relevant gymnastic theme might be used to reinforce what has been learned. There are a few important exceptions to this rule: lifting, carrying, pushing and pulling. Because these activities cause so many injuries, and because the techniques of carrying them out correctly are specific and exact, they should be taught precisely and directly in the gymnastic lessons. Further details will be found in Theme 47.

Observation

Teachers' observation and appreciation of what constitutes good movement must be well developed so that they can improve the quality of their children's work. The skill of observation will improve with practice, but in general terms teachers should frequently observe the whole class to ensure that they are all answering the given task as well as they can and that everything is safe. The way to do this is to walk around the outside of the class looking inwards. When teachers go to the middle of the hall - to help an individual child perhaps - they should remember that about half the class will be out of their sight. It sometimes pays to follow the action of a series of individuals for twenty seconds or so. It can also help a teacher's observation to make a running commentary to herself on the actions of individual children.

Children should also learn to observe other children's actions. They can be asked to observe and comment on other children's performances and criticise constructively. It is sometimes necessary, especially with younger children, to warn them what to look for before the movement takes place. Older children might also be expected to do a running commentary of their own and others' performances during the activities.

Clothing

It is important that children should change into the correct clothing for both safety and hygiene considerations. However, it is probably best for reception children to be expected only to take off their jackets and socks and shoes and to work barefoot. If they wear plimsolls, they should use the elasticated, not laced, type.

They should gradually be expected to change properly so that boys work in shorts and maybe a vest, while the girls wear pants and a blouse or a leotard. Skirts can be dangerous when a girl is working upside down as can long hair. Jewellery should never be worn for any physical activity.

Most teachers prefer their youngsters to work with bare feet if the floor is splinter-free because plimsolls prevent really skilful and fine footwork. Under no circumstances should children be allowed to work in stockinged feet.

Safety

Physical activities, by their very nature, contain a certain risk factor, but many educationists believe that children should gradually be exposed to this risk in order that they can learn to recognise it and to react sensibly to it.

The vast majority of children will not willingly attempt activities which they think are too difficult and therefore dangerous for them to perform unless specifically told to do so by a teacher, as can be the case with formal gymnastics. The teacher soon gets to know the very small minority who cannot recognise danger or who want to show off and she is able to take special precautions with them. In educational gymnastics children are expected to find their own answers to given problems and therefore this type of gymnastics can be taught very safely as long as some very obvious and simple criteria are met:

1 The teacher has an understanding through training of the subject.
2 The children are quiet, well behaved and respond promptly to instructions.
3 The children wear suitable clothing and footwear.
4 Tasks are set which can be answered by both the least able and the most able.
5 The teacher bears in mind the age and experience of her class when setting a task. This highlights the need for a school to follow and record a properly constructed scheme of work.
6 Work is normally learned on the floor before being applied to apparatus.
7 Children are trained to handle the apparatus efficiently.
8 The apparatus is specifically designed and constructed for gymnastics or similar physical activities. Stage blocks and the edge of a stage are often safe to use, but in general teachers should be wary of improvised apparatus.
9 The apparatus used is suitable for the individual theme being taught as well as for the age and experience of the children using it.
10 The apparatus is sited sensibly.
11 The apparatus is checked before use.
12 Mini-tramps and similar apparatus are used only by teachers expressly trained to use them.
13 There are no undue obstructions in the hall; the windows and light fittings are made of toughened materials or are suitably protected.
14 The floor and equipment are non-slip and splinter-free, especially if barefoot work is to be attempted.
15 Competent first aid is readily available.

Travelling on feet

It is extremely important that children enjoy physical education; their early experiences of the subject will affect their attitude towards it for a very long time. Some of them will be overawed when entering the hall for the first time and might wish to stand and observe for part or even all of the early lessons. They should be allowed to do so but be encouraged to take part, possibly being accompanied by an older child from the class.

Floorwork

Barefoot work will help children to run resiliently and softly on the balls of their feet. If teachers prefer their children to wear plimsolls, they should request parents to provide the laceless type.

Children often prefer to travel around the hall, all going in the same direction. Whereas this can sometimes be advantageous, even safer, e.g. when high speed is required, it is usually better to encourage children from the beginning to travel separately using their own pathway.

It is also important that children learn from the beginning to start and stop on the teacher's signal. A whistle should seldom if ever be required for its use often results in a noisy class. Instead the teacher should only need to say as quietly as possible 'Start now' or 'Stop'. Children should normally be expected to finish off their immediate work before stopping and then stand tall on the floor to look at the teacher.

Apparatus

The early lessons will probably be quite short on account of the inexperience of the children and the time taken to change. Consequently they might not contain apparatus work. When apparatus is used, it should be selected for its ease of handling and undemanding nature, e.g. mats, hoops, benches. If this is done, children can be taught how to carry apparatus and can be asked to check its correct positioning and safety before starting work (see passage on apparatus handling on page 7).

Especially in the early stages, children should be allowed to explore the apparatus in order to become confident of it. They will therefore wish to work on the apparatus for much of their time without using the floor around it as well. However, children should soon be taught that the floor and space around the apparatus is also to be used.

More often than not they should travel from the floor on to their piece of apparatus and then away from it before starting to use the same piece of apparatus again but probably from another starting point. Seldom should they remain for long on apparatus without using the floor under or around it. In this way, crawling about aimlessly on the apparatus is cut to a minimum, as are queues of waiting children.

Opening activities
1 Hold hands with a friend and walk about the hall to get to know it.
2 Trot about the hall clockwise and then change on a signal to anticlockwise.
3 Walk or trot about the hall to touch as many things as possible.

4

5

Floorwork
1 Find several ways of travelling, sometimes on both feet and sometimes on one.
2 Run here, there and everywhere without bumping into anyone.
3 Run here, there and everywhere without bumping into anyone but going quite close to them.
4 Walk in and out of each other first with noisy feet and then with quiet feet.
5 Run in and out of each other first with noisy feet and then with quiet feet.

6 Run about the hall stopping straight away when the teacher says 'and stop'.
7 Run on the spot and then, when the teacher says 'change', run about the hall and so on.
8 Walk and later trot about the hall, sometimes using very small steps and sometimes long steps.
9 Run about the hall slowly, and on a signal quickly, and so on.
10 Bounce about the hall sometimes on both feet and sometimes on one.
11 Skip in and out of each other.
12 Spring from one foot to the other about the hall.
13 Follow-my-leader about the hall with a friend.
14 Hold hands with a partner and find several ways of travelling about the hall on your feet.
15 Travel in and out of each other sometimes on the toes, sometimes on the heels, and sometimes on the edges of the feet.
16 Look at a space a short distance away and choose a way of travelling to it on your feet. Choose another way of travelling to the next space and so on.

17

18

Apparatus
1 Walk in and out and under the apparatus without touching it.
2 Move freely around the hall getting on and off any piece of apparatus that is not crowded.
3 Find various ways, using feet mainly, of getting on, travelling along and then getting off the apparatus.
4 Find several places to get on and to get off the apparatus using feet mainly.
5 Travel to as many places on the apparatus as you can using mostly your feet.

6

7

Closing activities
1 Move about the hall in as many different ways as you can think of.
2 Travel sometimes very close to the ground and sometimes tall in the air.
3 Find several new ways of walking.

4

5

Support theme
Directions

Travelling on hands and feet

The ability to take body weight on the hands is very important in gymnastics. Very few, if any, young children are able to take all their weight on their hands for any length of time, but they are able to distribute their weight on various combinations of hands and feet.

The ability to perform, for example, balances on the hands or cartwheel-type actions will come later when they have had experience of crawling activities, bunny hops, cartwheel-type actions, etc.

It will help greatly if children are encouraged to practise in their free time as well as during lesson time.

Opening activities
These can be described while the children are changing so that they start work as soon as they are ready. Good footwork should be stressed.

Floorwork
Good spacing and keeping the head up are important if collisions are to be avoided.

The children should be reminded that the body can take up a large space or a small space and that moving parts can go away from or towards or around the stationary parts.

Apparatus
Generally speaking, young children will become confident, and can therefore be taught to work with skill and verve, only on fairly low undemanding apparatus. This will be easily managed and children should be trained from the beginning to get it out and put it away for themselves.

Requests from the children to use the larger apparatus should be resisted. In this way, they will be able to explore fully the potential of small apparatus and in addition will look forward to using the large apparatus when they become older.

Children should be encouraged to travel sometimes with part of their weight on the apparatus and part on the floor.

Opening activities

1 Find three methods of travelling on feet only.
2 Run quietly in and out of each other and stop on the teacher's signal.
3 Skip in twos around the hall.

4

5

Floorwork

1 Travel about the hall on hands and feet in as many ways as you can think of.
2 Travel about the hall on hands and feet but without crawling.
3 Place your hands on the floor and jump your feet into the air.
4 Place your hands on the floor and jump your feet from side to side.
5 Place your feet on the floor and jump your hands from side to side.
6 Show how many ways you can bunny hop.
7 Show how many ways you can go from feet to hands to feet.
8 Try to balance on your hands.
9 Find ways of travelling on hands and feet with **a**) back facing the floor **b**) stomach facing the floor **c**) sides of body facing the floor.
10 Travel on hands and feet with only one hand and one foot moving at the same time with **a**) back facing the floor **b**) stomach facing the floor **c**) sides facing the floor.
11 Travel on hands and feet, first moving both hands at the same time, and then both feet with **a**) back facing the floor **b**) stomach facing the floor **c**) sides facing the floor.

12 Travel on **a**) two hands and one foot **b**) two feet and one hand.

13 Travel on hands and feet, one part only moving at any one time.

14 Travel on hands and feet with both feet or one foot going through the air.

15 Travel on hands and feet with **a**) head leading **b**) feet leading **c**) the side of the body leading.

16 Travel on hands and feet with **a**) hands and feet close together **b**) hands and feet far apart.

17 Travel on hands and feet, sometimes with feet moving around the hands, and sometimes hands moving around the feet.

18

19

Apparatus

1 Use hands and feet to get on and off the apparatus.

2 Use hands and feet to get on to, along or across, and off apparatus.

3 Travel as in 2 but sometimes with stomach, back or side uppermost.

4 Travel as in 2 but sometimes with head or feet leading.

5 Use hands and feet to get on to, along or across, and off the apparatus, and then travel in an interesting fashion to another piece of apparatus.

6

7

Closing activities

1 Hold hands with a partner and skip around the hall.

2 Slip steps around the hall.

3 Trot showing good style.

4

5

Support themes

1 Directions

2 Fast and slow

Theme 3

Travelling emphasising variety

The main aim of this work is firstly to continue giving children confidence in their own ability and enjoyment in exploiting it, and secondly to encourage them to think for themselves. Variety should be the outcome.

Opening activities

It is important that children become aware of where other children are, what they are doing and where they are going so that they will not interfere with each other's activities. They will find that with some vigorous activities, it is wiser for them all to travel clockwise or anticlockwise.

Floorwork

In order to 'throw out ideas' but to stop children from copying each other exactly it is better for the teacher to give a running commentary of what she sees happening (John is rolling, Mary is skipping, etc.) rather than asking the children to demonstrate. In this way also children keep working all the time and they keep quiet.

Apparatus

Simple, low and stable apparatus should be used with the gradual introduction of new pieces of apparatus which the children should be trained to handle properly.

Much depends on whether the teacher wants the children to work on their own apparatus for a few minutes before the whole team makes a change or prefers them to travel freely. Maybe a compromise of sometimes using one method and sometimes the other is best.

It is important that the children (and the teacher!) realise that the floor under and around the apparatus should be used constructively.

Queues might develop in early lessons but they should be reduced and stopped as a result of a) using the floor as well as the apparatus b) approaching and leaving the apparatus from different places.

Opening activities
1 Run about the hall, jump into the air, land and carry on running.
2 Walk then trot lightly around the hall, first in a clockwise direction, then anticlockwise.
3 Run about the hall skimming close to each other but never touching.
4 Bunny hop about the hall.

5

6

Floorwork
1 Visit many different parts of the hall, travelling forwards, backwards and sideways.
2 Find several methods of bouncing around the hall on different parts of your body.
3 Find several methods of darting around the hall.
4 Move around the hall using the hands to drag another part or parts of the body.
5 Travel in interesting and different ways gradually getting quicker and quicker before slowing right down.
6 Find methods of travelling other than by walking, running or crawling.
7 Put three parts of the body on the ground and travel a few metres on them. Repeat with another set of three parts.
8 Find several methods of rolling.

9 Find several methods of skipping around the hall.
10 Find three methods of travelling **a**) with the whole body very close to the ground **b**) with one part as high as possible.
11 Find several methods of travelling with the body **a**) as large as possible **b**) as small as possible.
12 Find several ways of travelling on your knees only, and later on elbows and knees.
13 Find several methods of travelling while holding hands with two friends.
14 Travel around the hall without hands and feet touching the floor.
15 Move in different ways keeping your body wide nearly all the time.
16 Move about in different ways but keeping your toes and hands pointed.
17 Step about the hall on various parts of the body.

18

19

Apparatus
1 Travel to every part of your apparatus finding different ways of moving on it.
2 Visit every piece of apparatus in the hall finding many ways of travelling on and between each piece.
3 Find as many places and ways as you can of getting on and off the apparatus.
4 Find several ways of travelling on the floor towards the apparatus, then on and along it and lastly away from it on the floor.

5

6

Closing activities
1 Pairs. Follow-my-leader about the hall.
2 Face a friend and hold hands. Find several ways of moving about the hall.
3 Balance in several different ways on two hands and a foot.

4

5

Support theme
Curving and straight pathways

Space

general in relation to the hall

By now, few children will be awed by the size of the hall. They should all be encouraged to work as individuals and be helped to realise the value of sometimes ranging all over the hall and apparatus, using large vigorous movements. There will be times, however, when they will wish to work in one location only, probably using small actions. They should also experience working sometimes close to the ground and sometimes as high as possible and safe.

Floorwork
The teacher can stipulate particular ways of travelling, probably from previous lessons.

In addition to stressing the importance of the best use of space, the teacher should coach for good quality movement and also wide variety.

Apparatus
Apparatus should be sited to allow children to approach from any direction. The teacher should encourage more than one child to be on the apparatus at any one time.

Children should not queue but should use the floor in a planned way so that they arrive on the apparatus when there is a suitable gap.

Opening activities
1 Bound around the hall, sometimes on both feet and sometimes on one foot.
2 Run around the hall very quietly, sometimes forwards and sometimes sideways.
3 Travel around the hall on hands and feet, sometimes very slowly and sometimes very quickly.
4 Run and jump to land facing another direction.

5

6

Floorwork
1 Travel all over the hall in interesting ways and touch various places on the floor and walls with various parts of the body.
2 Travel from one side of the hall to the other in an interesting way, then turn round and travel back in a new way and so on.
3 Travel from one end of the hall to the other and back again, sometimes on hands and feet and sometimes with other parts of the body touching the ground.
4 Travel in various ways, sometimes across, sometimes along and sometimes diagonally across the hall.
5 Move sometimes by stepping with various parts of the body and sometimes by rolling first in an anticlockwise direction and later in a clockwise direction. Later, do the same around your own imaginary circle.
6 Travel in as many ways as you can think of but keep facing one place all the time. After a short while, choose another place to face.
7 Visit every part of the hall, sometimes on feet, sometimes on hands and feet and sometimes in other ways.
8 Move all over the hall, sometimes keeping close to the floor and sometimes keeping part of you as near to the ceiling as you can.

9 Choose one part of the hall and move about in it in various ways but on one foot only. Choose another part of the hall and travel in it using other parts of the body and so on.
10 Visit everywhere in the hall for about half a minute, facing the outside all the time. Change to facing the middle all the time and so on.
11 Travel all over the hall, concentrating on changing the part of the body which is nearest to the ceiling.
12 Pairs. Take it in turns to lead your partner in interesting ways from one part of the hall to another part some distance away and so on.

13

14

Apparatus
1 Travel to every part of the hall, crossing each piece of apparatus as you come to it.
2 Move in an interesting way to a piece of apparatus and then get as near to the ceiling as you can. Then make your way off the apparatus and travel to another piece of apparatus and so on.
3 Move about on or hanging under your apparatus, sometimes keeping as close to the ground as you can and sometimes as close to the ceiling as you can.
4 Get on and off your apparatus at different places and in different ways.

5

6

Closing activities
1 Run around the hall and jump into the air, land quietly and stand still. Repeat.
2 In twos, follow your partner around the hall and copy what he does.
3 Walk with long strides and body close to the floor.

4

5

Support themes
1 Stopping and stillness
2 Curving and straight pathways

Weight bearing

By now, children will be very competent at taking their body weight on their feet, and to a lesser extent their hands, both when stationary and while moving. To become gymnasts, they must become more skilful at both of these, but they must also learn to use other parts of the body.

Nearly every part of the body is capable of taking the body weight and some provide a more stable base than others. Generally a wide base is more stable and stronger (if that is what is needed) than a narrow base, and rounded areas of the body sometimes need another part of the body to act as an 'outrigger'.

A high stretched position is usually harder to hold than a low one because its centre of gravity is higher.

Balancing on a high piece of apparatus, especially if it is narrow, always seems difficult, as does balancing on a moving piece of equipment.

The ability to take body weight on the hands is particularly important to aspiring gymnasts and frequent opportunities should be given for them to learn this skill.

This theme, by its very nature, tends to be taught statically. Balances should not usually be held for more than two or three seconds, during which time the child tries to improve his position. Travelling on or on to nominated body parts should play a large part in every lesson.

Lastly, if the children are very young, the teacher might prefer to say 'let both feet touch the ground', rather than 'take your weight on both feet'.

Floorwork
It normally pays to talk to the class while they are working rather than to stop them and talk. It sometimes helps children to concentrate on answering the task if they say aloud which part of the body is taking their weight.

Apparatus
Where no specific body parts are indicated, the teacher might start by leaving the choice open, and then gradually stipulate the different body parts.

Opening activities
1 Travel to visit every part of the hall.
2 Travel round the hall in sideways directions using various methods.
3 Move round the hall sometimes very quickly and sometimes very slowly.

4

5

Floorwork
1 Experiment to find how many parts of the body can bear your weight.
2 Find which parts of your body you can rest on and then take up **a)** different high balances **b)** different low balances.
3 Take body weight on various groups of three parts.
4 Take body weight on various groups of four parts.
5 Take body weight on various pairs of matching parts (e.g. feet, hands, knees).
6 Take body weight on various dissimilar parts (e.g. one elbow and one foot).
7 Take body weight on various areas or patches (e.g. bottom, back, chest). Reduce the size of the patch.
8 Take body weight on two different parts, one on the right side and one on the left side of the body. Find other answers to the task.
9 Take body weight on two parts, each on the same side. Find other answers to the task.

10 Take body weight on both feet **a)** far apart **b)** close together. Do the same on other matching parts.

11 **a)** Stand on both feet and move the hands in various directions in the air gently, then vigorously, while maintaining balance.
  b) Support body weight on another two parts, then move as in **a)**.

12 Balance on one leg. On how many other single parts can you balance?

13 Take body weight on two knees and 'walk'. On how many body parts can you walk?

14 Take body weight on three parts and 'walk' around the hall. Repeat on other combinations of three parts.

15 Spin on one foot. On which other single parts or patches can you spin?

16 Take up a balance on two parts. Slowly lower another part to the ground; lightly touch the floor before returning to the starting position. Repeat with other balances and lowering parts in varying directions.

17 Take up a wide balance and slowly stretch another part sideways until balance is nearly lost. Return to the starting position. Repeat with other balances, narrow as well as wide.

18 Stand on both feet and walk the hands around the feet. Repeat but take your weight on other parts.

19

20

Apparatus

1 Travel on the floor and apparatus stopping occasionally to balance on different body parts.

2 Travel on the floor and apparatus changing the body parts on which you travel.

3 Travel sometimes on two, three or four parts.

4 Find several places where you can place your hands on the apparatus and either jump your feet on to the apparatus as well, or over the apparatus and on to the floor the other side.

5

6

Closing activities

1 Move slowly round the hall, sometimes taking weight on hands and feet, sometimes rolling.

2 Walk and trot showing good style. Stop on a signal and stand showing a good position.

3 Pairs. One runs around the hall, sometimes slowly and sometimes quickly. His partner stays close behind.

4

5

Support theme
Simple body shapes

Rocking and rolling

Children love rocking and rolling – just look at them at play, especially on a grassy slope! Rolling is also an extremely important component of a child's gymnastic experience. Many teachers therefore include a rolling activity in most gymnastic lessons just as they include activities which involve taking weight on the hands.

In addition to giving them this regular practice, it pays to concentrate the children's minds by devoting the main activity of several lessons to rolling. However, because concentration on rolling over successive lessons can be painful, many teachers tend to devote one period to rolling activities and to return to the same theme after a gap of a week or two.

Although most rolling will take place on mats, there are advantages in getting children to roll on the floor as long as it is safe and clean; many rolling activities are quite comfortable, even on the hard floor, and the unrestricted space encourages interesting changes of direction and pathways.

However, some rolls, especially those which involve taking the body weight along the length of the spine, can be painful if repeated sufficiently often and therefore a plentiful supply of gymnastic mats is highly desirable. It is important that they are non-slip and can be placed next to each other without gaps developing.

Children should be trained to lift, and never drag, mats. Usually two or as many as four children are needed to move one mat. This is simplified if light-weight mats are provided, which even infants can cope with.

The storage of mats always presents difficulties, but few are designed to be rolled up or folded. Some mats are stiff and can be leaned against a wall and therefore take up less floor space. However they are stored, but especially if on top of each other on the floor, children must be trained to take their turn to collect their mat. Some groups could be expected to collect their mat before collecting their other pieces of apparatus, and some vice versa.

Recently, thick landing mats have become very popular. They can be extremely valuable for landings from apparatus but are not necessary for normal rolling activities. (As an aside, care should be taken that they are of the correct thickness and density if they are to be used for high jumping.)

Apparatus
There must be sufficient practice at floor level before rolling on apparatus. Children must be allowed to proceed at their own ability and confidence level.

Opening activities
1 Run, jump to land sometimes on both feet and sometimes on one foot.
2 Travel around the hall on hands and feet.
3 Dart in and out of each other, keeping at least a metre apart.

4

5

Floorwork
1 Rock on as many different parts of your body and in as many ways as you can (in curled and stretched positions).
2 Lie on your back and practise any rocking movement (in curled and stretched positions) a) forwards and backwards b) sideways c) diagonally.
3 Sit with hands or arms clasped behind the knees, rock forwards and backwards making the rocks progressively larger.
4 Lie on your stomach, practise any rocking movements a) forwards and backwards b) sideways.
5 Rock on other parts of the body than the back or the stomach.
6 Join together two or three different types of rock.
7 Lie on your back, rock forwards and backwards so that the body rotates like hands on a clock.
8 Rock and turn as in 6, but on other parts of the body.

9 Rock in a variety of ways; make the rocks progressively larger so that they result in a roll. Use your hands if it helps.

10 Roll in as many different ways as possible.

11 Roll sideways in a stretched position with the arms sometimes by the side, or 'above' the head, or crossed in front of the chest.

12 Crouch and roll in a curled position **a**) forwards **b**) sideways **c**) backwards **d**) diagonally.

13 Sit and roll in a curled position **a**) sideways **b**) backwards **c**) diagonally.

14 Stand with legs together. Bend your legs slowly to sink and roll away in various directions.

15 Stand and twist downwards to roll away.

16 Join several different rolls together. Repeat and improve the sequence.

17 Practise a variety of rolls which finish in a standing position.

18 Roll smoothly to stand and jump into the air.

19

20

Apparatus

1 Practise a variety of rolls along the apparatus. (Low broad apparatus should be used, e.g. benches, top section of a box, agility plank. It sometimes helps to lay a mat on top of the apparatus (in such a way that it will not slip). Children may need to be told that they can roll along the apparatus while part of their body is in contact with the ground.)

2 Take up a good starting position, approach the apparatus, jump on to it, roll along it and roll off it on to a mat whenever possible.

3 Circulate freely between pieces of apparatus, rolling on the first and under the next. (The movement between the apparatus is as important as that which is performed on the apparatus and should show variety and good style. Teachers could stipulate, in general terms, the method to be used.)

4 From a good starting position travel to the apparatus, roll on to it and along it before jumping off.

5 Approach the apparatus, travel along, under, across or over it and move away from it to a finishing position, with a roll somewhere.

6

7

Closing activities

1 Sit in a curled position and then sit up showing a good position.

2 Stand in a good position and then trot around the hall showing good style.

3 Take the weight on hands with high tails.

4

5

Support theme
Fast and slow

Theme 7

Bridges

For most of their time up until now, children have been travelling using methods which are so universal that they have their own names, for example, walking, running, jumping, bunny hops, rocking and rolling.

The lessons on weight bearing introduced children to thinking of positions and movements special to themselves. This theme is very easily understood and will take further the idea of personalising movement.

The emphasis in this theme must be on children finding many answers to each problem set, but equally they must choose a few answers and try to improve them. To do this, they must develop an awareness of what each part of their body is doing and develop a feeling within their body of getting a good position and improving on it. This is most easily done when the body is stationary, but teachers must aim to give children the experience of moving in, or into and through good positions as soon as they will benefit from it.

Some children might be able to perform short sequences of movement and to repeat them.

Apparatus

The apparatus should be suitable for the theme, i.e. stable and not very high.

When teachers are sure that children are confident it is important to check that they are answering the task set.

Some children might hang from the apparatus in bridge shapes, but care should be taken over safety before suggesting it to them.

Opening activities

1 Run on the spot, trot to a spot five metres away, run on the spot, and so on, sometimes forwards, sideways and backwards.
2 Move around the hall near the ground and then with one part very high.
3 Practise a favourite movement.

4

5

Floorwork

1 Make bridge shapes using various parts of the body to rest on.
2 Find several bridge shapes on **a)** two hands and two feet **b)** two feet and two elbows **c)** two hands and two heels. Hold each for a few seconds before changing.
3 Find several bridge shapes on **a)** two hands and a foot **b)** two feet and the forehead **c)** two knees and one other part.
4 Find several bridge shapes on **a)** a hand and a foot **b)** a knee and a foot **c)** a foot and another part.
5 Find balances on a variety of **a)** four parts **b)** three parts **c)** two parts **d)** a patch of the body and other parts.
6 Move from one bridge shape to another by turning.
7 Find three high bridge shapes and three low bridge shapes.
8 Find two bridge shapes and travel along in them by, for example, 'walking' or 'jumping'.
9 Travel two metres by twisting from one bridge shape into another.
10 Stand tall and then lower gently various parts of the body into a bridge position (if possible forwards, sideways and backwards).
11 Take up high balances and then lower different parts of the body to form a bridge.

12 Think of a good bridge shape and find several ways of moving into it. Repeat with other bridges.
13 Take up a good bridge shape and find several ways of getting up from it. Repeat with other bridges.
14 Lie on the floor and push up into a bridge. Repeat using other low starting positions.
15 Move between several different bridge shapes by rolling.
16 Find a variety of bridge shapes with different parts of the body high.
17 Find a variety of wide, narrow and long bridge shapes.
18 Find a bridge shape on four parts. Keep two parts on the ground and walk the other two parts around. Repeat using other starting positions.

19

20

Apparatus
1 Move on or about the apparatus in various ways, finding interesting bridge shapes to take up in different places.
2 Move on the apparatus in or through bridge shapes.
3 Move to the apparatus, along the apparatus and lastly on the floor away from the apparatus in or through bridge shapes.
4 Lower the body in various ways from the apparatus to make bridges on the floor.

5

6

Closing activities
1 Move around the hall as lightly as possible.
2 Trot, jump in the air and make a good landing - continue.
3 Hold hands with a partner and skip in and out of other pairs.

4

5

Support theme
Wide, narrow, high, low body shapes

Curling, stretching and arching

The children have previously enjoyed the experience of travelling in various ways and of taking their weight on different parts, and are now ready to explore how the body can change shape while either on the spot or while moving. Curling, stretching and arching are part of their normal lives but seldom are they done to extremes. It is this feeling and appreciation of real stretch, real curl and real arch that children should experience, first in a held position with the body supported on various bases and later while moving. Curling is normally considered to be a movement towards the centre of the body resulting in a tucked (ball-like) shape; stretching is concerned with movements away from the centre (long and wide); while arching is concerned with hyper-extension, normally backwards or sideways (no tuck position can be involved). Real stretching, curling and arching take place mainly in the torso. However, the stretch action of the limbs and the body extremities (usually fingers and toes but, depending on the body position, also elbows, knees, etc.) should also be stressed when teaching stretching and arching action. In curling, the action of the head and neck should also be stressed.

As with other themes, teachers will sometimes be explicit about what they expect their children to do, e.g. 'stretch upwards, then sideways', and sometimes will expect them to experiment as a result of an instruction like 'stretch in as many directions as you can'.

Apparatus

Infants and lower juniors can work to advantage with mats, canes and hoops, skipping ropes on the floor, benches, individual layers of a box, rostrum, etc., before using larger pieces of apparatus. The children should not be expected or asked to maintain a fully curled or stretched position for a lengthy time but rather to alternate between the two positions.

Opening activities

1 Travel around the hall on hands and feet in a variety of ways.
2 Trot and jump into the air concentrating on quiet landings.
3 Walk, trot, then run around the hall forwards, sideways and backwards.

4

5

Floorwork

1 How many different ways can you curl, stretch and arch your whole body? (The children should be asked what is meant by 'curl, stretch and arch'.)
2 Stand in various positions on both feet; stretch, curl and arch your whole body in as many ways as you can.
3 Lie on your back, side and front and find many ways of stretching, curling and arching your whole body.
4 Take up various bridge positions first on four parts, then three, then two parts, finding several ways of curling, stretching and arching on each.
5 Take your weight on one part or limb of the body and find several ways of stretching, curling and arching. Change to balancing on another part.
6 Take up various patch balances and find ways of curling, stretching or arching.
7 Take up various body positions and try to a) curl one part and stretch another b) arch the spine and stretch or curl other parts of the body.

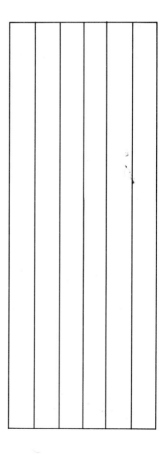

8 Think of a stretched position and find ways of moving through it. Do the same with other stretched and curled positions. (For example, a gymnast might select a semi-curled bridge position on hands and feet with stomach facing the floor. He could travel through this position by first standing, then falling under control on to his hands before rolling out of the position sideways. Likewise there are countless ways of passing through a balance on hands or a crab position.)

9 Travel on the floor a short distance and move through two or three stretched and curled positions.

10 Travel on both feet with the body stretched **a)** as wide as possible **b)** as tall as possible **c)** curled tightly.

11 Take up a wide bridge shape on four or three parts and travel five metres in that shape.

12 Take up a long bridge shape on four or three parts and travel in that shape.

13 Roll **a)** in a tight curled shape **b)** in a long stretched shape.

14 Travel from feet to another weight-bearing part, e.g. seat, shoulders, back, with body **a)** curled **b)** stretched and so on.

15 Stand and jump into the air showing various stretched shapes in the air.

16 Trot and jump into the air, showing various stretched shapes in the air.

17

18

Apparatus
1 Travel across, over, under, in, out and along the apparatus in a variety of ways, sometimes showing a stretch, sometimes a curl and sometimes an arch.

2 Travel sometimes on the apparatus and sometimes on the floor concentrating on travelling through stretched or curled positions.

3 Travel to the apparatus, arrive on it in a curled position, leave it showing a stretch.

4 Find places where the body can hang from the apparatus or can be supported by the floor and the apparatus in **a)** stretched shapes **b)** curled shapes.

5

6

Closing activities
1 Bounce around the hall forwards, sideways and backwards.
2 Practise a favourite movement.
3 Hold hands with a friend and walk, then trot, in and out of other pairs.

4

5

Support themes
1 Fast and slow
2 Direction

Theme 9

Jumping emphasising good landings

Flying through the air is very exciting and should form a substantial part of every child's physical education. Jumping is the easiest method of achieving flight. It is important, however, that the children learn to land safely from a whole variety of actions.

The exact technique of landing will depend on the jump and the movement to follow, e.g. the landing from a high jump will differ from the landing from a jump involving a turn; again they will both differ if they are to be followed by either another jump or a roll. However, in the first stages, single jumps only should be performed.

Landing will normally involve reaching out for the floor and landing on the balls of the feet which will be pointing forwards and not very far apart. The ankles and knees will give in order to absorb the shock and gradually slow down the speed of the body. The amount of knee bend will depend mainly on the height of the jump and children should experiment to find the degree of bend required. It is normally wise to err on the side of bending too much rather than too little, but there is little point in bending the knees fully if there is no need to do so. It is usual for the upper body to be kept fairly upright with the head held high; the bottom goes down towards the heels and the knees forwards but the chin should not be allowed to hit the knees.

This theme concentrates mainly on teaching good safe landings to stop from single jumps. The techniques involved are very different from those when a gymnast lands from a jump and immediately bounces up again into another jump. When children perform consecutive jumps in the theme, it is important that they land fairly deeply in between jumps. They should be asked to experiment in order to discover the best landings for the particular movements involved.

Apparatus

It is important to choose the best apparatus for the task to be set. Nervous children should not be made to jump from too great a height or from unstable apparatus. Mats are not normally required for small jumps and in any case do little to absorb landing shocks. Care must be taken that they do not slide and that their siting does not restrict the amount of landing spots and take-off spots which the children can choose; it would be ideal in most cases if mats could be provided all round the apparatus.

Opening activities

1 Skip or trot in twos about the hall following your partner.
2 Practise a favourite movement which involves travelling.
3 Move in interesting ways, visiting all parts of the hall.
4 Travel from feet on to hands and back on to feet again in several different ways.

5

6

Floorwork

1 Perform single small jumps on the spot, landing on both feet. Concentrate not on the jump but on a resilient landing. When competent, increase the height.
2 Perform consecutive jumps on the spot off and on to both feet. Concentrate on good landings.
3 Perform single standing jumps, forwards, then sideways and lastly backwards.
4 Perform consecutive standing jumps forwards, then sideways and lastly backwards. Concentrate on resilient but firm landings.
5 As in 3 and 4, but increase the length of the jump.
6 Trot slowly, take off one foot and land on both feet, concentrating on a good landing a) gradually make the jump higher b) gradually trot more quickly and make the jump longer.

26

7 Run and jump over a mark on the floor.
8 Run and jump to land on a mark on the floor.
9 Trot slowly and jump to turn clockwise and anticlockwise through
  a) 45° **b)** 90° **c)** 180°. Concentrate on a good landing on both feet.
10 Jump **a)** forwards **b)** sideways **c)** backwards from one foot to the
  other. Concentrate on good landings.
11 Perform various consecutive jumps on one foot only around the hall
  a) forwards **b)** backwards **c)** sideways. Change feet.
12 Trot, jump and turn in the air to land safely on one foot.

13

14

Apparatus
1 Jump over a variety of apparatus to land well. (Mats, canes, ropes,
  benches, single layers of boxes and other low, stable apparatus;
  children should approach from various positions.)
2 Travel in an interesting way on the floor to the apparatus, get on to
  it neatly and find various places along which and off which to
  jump. Concentrate on resilient landings and gradually jumping
  from greater heights. (Larger, stable apparatus also should be
  used.)
3 Find suitable places where you can jump over the apparatus, or *up*
  and off the apparatus, or jump on to it and off it in one continuous
  movement. (Mats, canes, ropes, benches, single layers of boxes and
  other low, stable apparatus; children should approach from various
  positions.)
4 Move on the floor and the apparatus practising a variety of
  interesting jumps. (Larger stable apparatus also should be used.)

5

6

Closing activities
1 Roll, sometimes with a stretched body, sometimes with a curled
  body.
2 Travel on hands and feet, sometimes forwards, sometimes
  sideways.
3 Bunny hops with high tails.

4

5

Support theme
Shapes in the air

Stopping and stillness

Children seldom think of stopping and being still as a positive act; they might stop in order to observe other children's work and they might keep still because they are tired; they certainly learn to stop and keep still when the teacher tells them to do so and, somewhat as an aside, this theme will help teachers in this process.

It is now time for children to learn that stopping and being still has a positive value. Sometimes it is used at the beginning of an action or part way through it in order to prepare both mind and body for ensuing action; sometimes it is used to signify the end of an action or series of actions; sometimes it is used as a planned contrast to action.

During these moments of stillness children should concentrate on holding good body positions and planning their ensuing movements. Later in their gymnastic experience, children will learn to balance in much more difficult and interesting ways and these will serve as extremely telling components of their sequences.

As with some other early themes, this work might only last for two periods but can be returned to occasionally when thought to be necessary.

Floorwork

The technique of stopping will depend on the movement which precedes it, but it usually entails reaching out for the ground when height or speed is involved. From a jump, for instance, either one or both legs reach forwards before landing and then absorb the body's momentum, or immediately the person lands, one leg is thrust forwards to absorb the momentum.

Generally, the children should be asked to plan their own actions, including stopping. If they are to stop on the teacher's signal, they should be warned beforehand. They can then experiment to find the effect of travelling at different speeds. They can also listen for the signal and prepare themselves. It is good experience for them to be required, on occasion, to stop on a signal without having been warned previously.

Apparatus

Simple positions of stillness on the floor can become difficult balances when performed on apparatus. The apparatus used should allow for safe moments of stillness.

Opening activities
1 Run and jump around the hall.
2 Move freely and fairly quickly to visit all parts of the hall.
3 Hold a partner's hand and skip around the hall.
4 Travel around the hall, first on 1, and then 2, finally 3 parts.
5 Practise 4 ways of travelling on feet only.

6

7

Floorwork
1 Travel about the hall in many different ways, stopping and keeping still on the words 'and stop'.
2 Look at a space five metres away. Either walk or run to it and stop in a good standing position.
3 Walk or trot around the hall. Stop and stand still every few seconds.
4 Trot in and out of each other. Every few seconds, trot towards a friend and stop about a metre away from him. Pass to one side of him and continue.
5 Run around the hall stopping every now and again a) slowly b) very suddenly.
6 Run sometimes slowly, sometimes very quickly, and stop immediately on the teacher's signal.
7 Walk slowly around the hall using very long strides. Stop and keep still every few seconds, sometimes part way through a stride.

8 Travel as in **6**, but stop immediately on the teacher's signal.
9 Run at various speeds to jump. On landing stop and keep still.
10 Run at various speeds to jump. On landing jump immediately into the air again and land on the same spot to keep still.
11 Stand on one foot, or sit on the floor. Spin round and allow your movement to slow down and stop naturally. Later stop the spinning early.
12 Move from a curled position into a stretched position and hold it for a second. Continue.
13 Join three different rolls together. Repeat the sequence in order to memorise it. Repeat but with a held position for a second or so between or during each roll.
14 Travel for ten seconds in a bridge shape. Stop and keep still for a few seconds before travelling in another bridge shape.
15 Roll from a wide bridge shape into a narrow bridge shape and hold for a few seconds; roll into another wide shape; continue.
16 Travel around the hall on feet only, stopping the action regularly every second (as in a jerky old film).
17 Travel as in **16** but on other parts of the body.
18 Hold hands with a partner and travel in various ways about the hall. Stop in time with each other.

19

20

Apparatus
1 Travel on the floor to the apparatus and jump over it. Land and keep still for a second or so before travelling back under or over the apparatus using a different method.
2 Travel freely on the apparatus finding interesting and differing positions of stillness on various parts of the body.
3 From a good starting position on the floor travel on to the apparatus. Hold a good balance there for a few seconds and return to your starting position. Repeat from other places.
4 Travel as in **4**, but having held a still position on the apparatus, continue in the same direction of travel to a finishing position on the floor.

5

6

Closing activities
1 Skip rhythmically around the hall.
2 Travel backwards using different methods of moving.
3 Take up a bridge position on hands and feet. Push up on to fingers and toes. Repeat with another bridge position on hands and feet.

4

5

Support theme
Travelling forwards, sideways and backwards

Theme 11

Space

personal

Children should be reminded that previously (Theme 4) they have visited and worked in many spaces within the hall (general space). They should now think in terms of their own bubble of space and should discover ways of working within it.

They can either occupy a large or small part of their personal space. They can also move within it in a variety of ways: for example, they can move towards or away from the centre of their space; they can move around its periphery; they can work near or far away from the ground.

When children have explored their personal bubble of space while remaining on the spot, they can do the same while moving either on the floor or on the apparatus or in flight.

Apparatus
The children should be reminded to use different starting and finishing locations.

Opening activities
1 Run in and out of each other, changing direction in order to prevent a collision, or on a signal from the teacher.
2 Move into spaces using a different type of jump each time.
3 Take weight on hands with hips high.

4

5

Floorwork
1 Travel by various methods to spaces in the hall, and take up a different shape at each space.
2 Stand with legs comfortably apart, discover how far forwards, backwards, sideways, upwards and downwards you can reach with a) one hand b) both hands c) an elbow d) the head.
3 Stand on one foot and perform as in 2 above.
4 Balance on shoulders and explore your bubble of space with your feet.
5 Sit and explore your bubble of space with hands and feet.
6 Kneel and explore your bubble of space with one then both hands.
7 Take up various bridge shapes and explore your own bubble of space.
8 Take up a bridge shape occupying a large amount of space. Move around in this position.
9 Take up a comfortable standing position, stretch out into space as far as possible and then curl up into a very small space before stretching out in another direction.
10 Run a few paces and jump into the air to discover how many areas of your bubble of space can be reached first by hands, then feet and lastly hands and feet.
11 Perform a variety of rolls, some occupying a large and some a small amount of space.
12 Travel two metres from a standing position occupying a large space into another position occupying a small space. Continue.
13 Place your hands on the floor. Move in as many ways as you can without moving your hands. Repeat, but with feet fixed.

14 Take your body weight on various parts of the body and then explore your bubble of space with other parts of the body a) around the outside edges of it b) across it c) towards or away from your centre.

15

16

Apparatus
1 Move on the apparatus or hanging from it or partly on the apparatus and partly on the floor. Change from a position which takes up a lot of space to one which takes up very little.
2 Travel about the apparatus and surrounding floor on feet only. Sometimes move with the hands stretched very high and sometimes with them stretched out sideways a long way.
3 Travel about the apparatus and surrounding floor on various parts of the body. Stretch one or both legs as high into the air or as far sideways as you can as often as you can.

4

5

Closing activities
1 Practise various jumps and turns in the air followed by good landings.
2 Roll about the hall in different directions and at different speeds.
3 Take up a bridge position, roll into another and so on.

4

5

Support theme
Curling, stretching and arching

Theme 12

Directions

forwards, backwards, sideways, diagonally

The *direction* in which a gymnast travels (horizontally or vertically) and the *pathway* he follows (a direct pathway or an indirect pathway) to his destination both influence strongly the way in which he moves. These factors are very closely intertwined in all movements and so, in order to avoid confusion, each is introduced separately as follows: directions, horizontal - Theme 12, directions, vertical - Theme 20, pathways - Theme 24, various combinations - Themes 29, 35, 40, 50.

Floorwork
At all times an atmosphere of co-operation is essential when a group works in a confined space. Each person, while concentrating on his own actions, must be aware of what others are doing in order to be able to take avoiding action by changing his/her own speed, direction or pathway.

Apparatus
Particular care should be taken with dismounts; backward ones can be too difficult in some circumstances for some young children, although in some cases they can be easier than forward dismounts. Children should gradually be expected to think about what they are going to do before they actually do it. Young children can be expected to plan for about ten seconds' work and older children the whole sequence.

Opening activities
1 Run and jump in a variety of ways.
2 Follow your partner in twos.
3 Bunny hops and rolls.

4

5

Floorwork
1 Travel on various parts of the body in many different directions.
2 Run, skip, stride, slip step, hop, bounce **a**) forwards **b**) backwards **c**) sideways **d**) diagonally forwards **e**) diagonally backwards.
3 Travel as in **2**, changing direction on a signal.
4 Travel on hands and feet, sometimes with stomach, or back, or side uppermost **a**) forwards **b**) backwards **c**) sideways **d**) diagonally forwards **e**) diagonally backwards.
5 Move in various ways along a straight line to a destination ten metres away, but change direction on a signal.
6 Perform various types of jumps **a**) forwards **b**) backwards **c**) sideways **d**) diagonally forwards **e**) diagonally backwards.
7 Join together two different jumps forwards, then two jumps sideways, and lastly one jump backwards.
8 Travel from feet to hands to feet **a**) forwards **b**) sideways **c**) diagonally backwards **d**) diagonally forwards.
9 Travel in a variety of bridge shapes **a**) forwards **b**) backwards **c**) sideways **d**) diagonally forwards **e**) diagonally backwards.
10 Run forwards and jump. Land and then run and jump in a sideways direction. Continue.
11 Run forwards and jump, turn in the air and land. Continue.
12 Move from one bridge shape to another by curling and stretching various parts of the body, sometimes in one direction and sometimes in another.

13 Lower the body from a standing position forwards, then backwards and lastly sideways to a balance on the shoulders. Move in the same direction back to standing.

14 Join together several rolls, each in a different direction.

15 Pairs. One travels using simple methods but changing direction frequently. Partner tries to follow.

16

17

Apparatus

1 Approach the apparatus, travel along it, off it and away from it, sometimes forwards and sometimes in other directions. (Mats, benches, canes, ropes, small trestles, boxes and planks and other low apparatus.)

2 Travel forwards along, over, under or across the apparatus. Repeat where possible and safe by travelling **a**) backwards **b**) sideways **c**) diagonally forwards. (Mats, benches, canes, ropes, small trestles, boxes and planks and other low apparatus.)

3 Move forwards and travel along a piece of apparatus, travel sideways to the next piece and go sideways along it, travel backwards to and along the next. Continue. (Larger apparatus could be used here in addition to low apparatus.)

4 Approach the apparatus moving forwards, and leave apparatus going backwards or sideways. (Children should be encouraged to repeat several times, and to improve each selected series of movements.)

5

6

Closing activities

1 Skip, weaving in and out of each other, gradually speeding up and then slowing down to stop.

2 Find several ways of taking weight on the hands.

3 Roll, balance, roll, balance and so on.

4

5

Support themes

1 Stopping and stillness

2 General space in the hall

Theme 13

Limbs together and apart

This theme is concerned with increasing children's body awareness - an essential to good movement. By asking children to work with their arms and legs sometimes together and sometimes apart, teachers will focus attention on individual body parts and the effect of their relationships. For example, running with small strides is very different from running with large strides and they should be used to serve different purposes; teachers should ensure that children become aware of the differences.

Apparatus

If, up to the present, the children have been allowed to move freely from apparatus to apparatus, now might well be the time to organise them into groups of about five, to allocate them to certain pieces of apparatus and to rotate the groups every few minutes.

Children should be reminded that their weight need not always be on their hands and feet. They could for instance be on shoulders and hands with feet in the air or on any patches of the body. Likewise, they need not be on top of the apparatus all the time. They could hang from it or have their weight partly on the apparatus and partly on the floor.

Opening activities

1 Walk around the hall sometimes taking your weight from heel to toe and sometimes on the ball of the feet only.
2 Travel around the hall using several different methods.
3 Run and jump to turn in mid-air and land and jump again immediately.

4

5

Floorwork

1 Travel about the hall in various ways, concentrating at first on having arms sometimes far apart and sometimes close together, and later, on having legs sometimes far apart and sometimes together.
2 Walk in various directions sometimes with giant steps and sometimes with very small steps.
3 Bounce around the hall forwards, backwards and sideways with **a)** feet together **b)** feet far apart **c)** arms together **d)** arms apart.
4 Balance on the shoulders and elbows with the legs in the air. Alternate between putting the legs close together in various directions and putting them far apart in various directions.
5 Balance on different parts of the body **a)** with legs together or apart **b)** with arms together or apart.
6 Take up a bridge shape on hands and feet. Travel around with **a)** legs sometimes far apart and sometimes close together **b)** hands sometimes far apart and sometimes together.
7 Run and jump **a)** with legs close together in mid-air **b)** with legs apart in mid-air **c)** changing in mid-air.
8 Stand with legs comfortably apart and find how many ways the arms can be stretched **a)** together **b)** far away.

9 Take up a bridge shape on hands and feet. 'Walk' around with hands sometimes close to feet and sometimes far away.
10 Find various ways of travelling around the hall with a) legs either far apart or together b) arms either far apart or together c) arms far away from legs or near to them.
11 Stand with arms and legs wide apart. Turn the body to face the other way, first keeping arms and legs far apart all the time and then bringing them close to the body in the middle of the turn.
12 Do the same as in 11 but with a jump.
13 Do the same as in 11 but spinning on one foot.
14 Do the same as in 11 and 12 but starting in various bridges.

15

16

Apparatus
1 Move on the apparatus and the surrounding floor to take up a whole variety of balance positions with a) the legs b) the hands being either far apart or close together.
2 Find various ways of mounting and dismounting from the apparatus with a) the legs b) the hands being either far apart or together.
3 Find various ways of either hanging from the apparatus or sharing the body weight between the apparatus and the floor while concentrating on having the body parts far apart or together.
4 Travel on the apparatus and the surrounding floor moving through various wide, long or narrow body shapes.

5

6

Closing activities
1 Run lightly here and there keeping at least a metre away from anyone else.
2 Bunny jump around the hall.
3 Practise a favourite movement.

4

5

Support themes
1 Direction
2 Stopping and stillness

Theme 14

Space

general in relation to the apparatus

In Theme 4, children were helped to use all the space in the hall and this will have been reinforced during most of the following lessons.

When children first use apparatus, they normally travel on top of it; they seldom consciously use the space all around it, i.e. above, below, to its sides and ends and between individual parts of it.

The intention in this theme is to help them think about the space around the apparatus and to discover how to make imaginative and good use of it. Children should also be encouraged to use all the apparatus. To take one example, it is very easy, if help is not given, for children to use only the planks or somersault bars and not the trestles supporting them.

In order to make full use of the space around the apparatus, children will learn that they need not always be in contact with the apparatus; they might, for example, be in flight over it or be on the floor near to it.

They will also learn that they can keep changing their spatial relationship with the apparatus by twisting in and out, turning or spinning around, curling and stretching, jumping, etc. However, the method of travel is not as important at this stage as the way in which space is used although the teacher might find it advisable sometimes to stipulate in general terms how the children are to move.

One bonus which should result from work on this theme is that queues of children waiting to work on apparatus should be eliminated; because all the space on and around the apparatus can be used, many children can be working at the same time.

Most of the lesson will be taught with the apparatus out, but it is important that the children are first warm and supple. Several minutes should therefore be spent on the opening activities on smaller equipment before getting out the larger apparatus.

This might be a good time for teachers to devote a little longer than usual to the best procedures and methods of moving, erecting, dismantling, checking and storing apparatus.

Opening activities
1 Run and jump around the hall.
2 Move freely and fairly quickly to visit all parts of the hall.
3 Hold a partner's hand and skip around the hall.
4 Travel around the hall, first on one, then two and finally three parts.
5 Practise four ways of travelling on feet only.
6 Move from feet to hands to feet and so on.

7

8

Apparatus
A *Using mats, canes, hoops, ropes, etc., spread out on the floor*
1 Find interesting ways of travelling over the equipment without touching it.
2 Find interesting ways of travelling from one piece of equipment to other pieces without touching the ground in between.
3 Find good ways of crossing pieces of equipment taking weight on one or both hands.
4 Travel in exciting ways around a piece of equipment and then across it and away to another piece and so on.

B *Using larger apparatus*

5 Travel freely in and out of the apparatus without touching it; sometimes go very close to the apparatus, sometimes as far away as possible from it and sometimes go straight for it, before changing pathway at the last moment.

6 Use different and interesting methods to travel to all pieces of the apparatus. Sometimes travel over the apparatus and sometimes under it. Sometimes touch the apparatus and sometimes do not.

7 Travel all over your apparatus stopping either to balance on top of it or be suspended from part of it.

8 Travel all over your apparatus finding as many different places as possible to mount and dismount.

9 Stand on the floor three or four metres away from the apparatus. Travel stylishly to the apparatus, along or across it, and then away from it to take up a good finishing position three or four metres away; travel in straight lines if possible. Move to another starting place and repeat.

10 Find places on the apparatus around which you can turn or twist. Some pieces will be horizontal, some vertical and some sloping.

11 Approach the apparatus and mount a low part of it. Travel on it to gradually gain height. Dismount if possible from a high part.

12 Travel on the apparatus keeping as low as possible and touching the floor if necessary.

13 Travel all over the apparatus. Stop every now and again to balance with a part of the body as far away from the apparatus as possible; the chosen part may be above, below or to one side of the apparatus.

14

15

Closing activities

1 Roll into a good balance. Roll into another balance and so on.
2 Move sideways using different methods of travel.
3 Travel smoothly from one bridge position to another.

4

5

Support themes

1 Stipulated methods of travelling or weight bearing
2 Personal space

Theme 15

Shape

long, wide, curled

Children should be aware at any time of their body shape, which can be put into four basic categories: 1) long and narrow, 2) wide, 3) curled, 4) twisted. They can recognise other people's shapes more easily than their own and so should be given the opportunity now and again of observing each other's work.

The body's shape is the result of the movement which led up to it. Sometimes this shape is held for a short while, either on the spot as in a balance, or travelling as in a jump or a roll. It is easiest to teach the concept of body shape through held positions on the spot and then progress to those held on the move.

Most of the time a gymnast's body shape is changing constantly. The shape at any fraction of time is extremely important to his action as far as both efficiency and style are concerned. This aspect of body shape is obviously the most difficult to put across, but it is also the most important. Probably the easiest way to approach it is to concentrate first on the gymnast adopting a good starting position and then passing through two contrasting shapes to finish in a good position. When this has been accomplished, the teacher could attempt to make the gymnast aware of his body shape at all times.

Floorwork
If the teacher observes the various body shapes used by children and comments aloud on them while they are working, this will give the children a variety of ideas and will ensure that they work quietly in order to hear her.

Apparatus
Apparatus work gives children the opportunity to practise a greater range of body shapes than does floorwork because, for example, the time in the air is increased when jumping from height; also swinging on ropes or gripping on to the apparatus enables children to balance upside down more easily.

Opening activities
1 Practise a favourite movement.
2 Travel around the hall on hands and feet.
3 In twos, dodge and mark around the hall.

4

5

Floorwork
1 Move about the hall showing as many different shapes as you can.
2 Move on to different parts of the body making large stretches
   a) which are flat b) which are not flat.
3 Take up a standing position, make a variety of good a) wide
   b) long and narrow c) curled d) twisted shapes. (The body
   extremities as well as knees and elbows are the easiest parts to
   concentrate on, but it is important that the feeling of stretch, curl,
   etc., be felt in the torso.)
4 Lie on the back, front or side. Make a variety of shapes.
5 Start from a variety of bridge positions. Make many different
   shapes.
6 Run and jump to make various a) wide b) long and narrow
   c) curled d) twisted shapes in mid-air. (Concentrate first on
   stretched jumps. Care must be taken to ensure that children do not
   rotate forwards or backwards (somersault) when tucked up tight in
   mid-air. This can usually be prevented by keeping heads high and
   not tucking very tightly.)

7 Travel around the hall on various body parts keeping **a**) the feet apart **b**) the feet together.

8 Travel around the hall in a variety of wide, long and narrow, curled and twisted shapes.

9 Perform three consecutive jumps, the first wide, the second long, and the third twisted.

10 Take up a variety of wide bridge shapes on hands and feet, walk the hands right around the feet wherever possible and keep a wide shape. (Clockwise and anticlockwise. Sometimes stomach, back or side uppermost.)

11 Take up a variety of bridge shapes on hands and feet, walk the feet round the hands as far as possible.

12 Take up a wide shape, roll into and hold a narrow shape and then rotate one part of the body to take up a twisted shape.

13 Travel from feet to hands to feet, changing shape from time to time.

14 Invent and practise a five-second sequence which involves travelling through a wide bridge shape.

15 Travel around the hall by rolling, jumping and step-like actions, making or passing through various body shapes. (The term 'step-like actions' may have to be investigated by the children. Of course, these actions exclude rolls, spins, sliding, jumping, etc.)

16 Find a variety of balances with the feet above the head showing wide, long, curled and twisted shapes.

17

18

Apparatus

1 Travel about the apparatus to find places where a variety of shapes can be held on top of, hanging from, or 'leaning against' it.

2 Travel through the air on to, over, along or off the apparatus showing many different shapes in the air. (Children must be capable of doing this safely.)

3 Move on the floor to the apparatus, on it, and on the floor away from it concentrating on travelling *through* contrasting shapes.

4

5

Closing activities

1 Pairs. Travel over and under each other in different ways.

2 Run, jump and turn round in the air to land and carry on running.

3 Take your weight on your hands and lower your legs to a different place.

4

5

Support themes

1 Directions

2 Weight bearing

Theme 16

Space

in relation to each other

School halls are never big enough! There will be occasions when half of the class will have to sit out so that there is enough space for the rest to perform a particularly energetic activity. Normally, however, the whole class will be working at the same time, and so it is important that children learn to work in close proximity. This will require an awareness of what their friends are doing and where they are going, while at the same time they themselves concentrate on performing their own movement as well as they can. They might have to slow down or speed up, or change direction, or even lift a body part to allow someone else to go underneath them - all good training for sympathetic relationships.

This theme also has a more positive role in that it introduces the idea of children working together to produce combined gymnastics. To do this they must first learn to observe each other while working themselves, so as to be able to assess each other's abilities and intentions. Early themes involve pairs of gymnasts reacting to each other without physical contact, but in later themes children will be expected to plan and execute quite advanced group sequences.

Floorwork
In many of the activities no mention has been made of how children should move but only of their interrelationships. Teachers should specify the method of moving according to the class's ability.

When working in pairs or fours, children must concentrate on their partner's actions but should also be aware of what any other person in their vicinity is doing.

Opening activities
1 Run about the hall concentrating on lightness.
2 Travel about the hall sometimes quickly and sometimes slowly.
3 Travel about the hall taking weight on hands frequently.

4

5

Floorwork
1 Travel forwards in an out of each other visiting every part of the hall and making sure that your bubble of space never touches anyone else's.
2 Travel on various parts of the body zigzagging around the hall in a clockwise direction.
3 Travel on various parts of the body zigzagging around the hall, half going clockwise and half anticlockwise.
4 Travel in and out of each other on various parts of the body but passing as close as possible without actually touching. (Children could run for a space and then skim past someone by turning a shoulder.)
5 Half the class travels fairly slowly on various parts of the body across the hall and back again. The other half works lengthwise. Contact must never take place!
6 Pairs. One travels on feet about the hall changing activity and direction every now and again. Partner copies keeping **a**) about two metres behind **b**) about five metres behind.
7 Pairs. A takes up a good bridge shape. B takes up various shapes that go well with A's. Change over.

8 Pairs. A takes up a good bridge shape. B travels under, over and around him.
9 Pairs. A travels slowly in a good bridge shape. B travels under, over and around him.
10 Pairs. Both roll in a variety of ways, sometimes very close to each other and sometimes two or three metres away.
11 Pairs. Starting five metres apart, travel slowly towards each other, take up a stretched balance on one foot, turn round and part.
12 Pairs. Starting five metres apart, find ways of travelling towards each other, meeting and parting.
13 Fours. Working inside a small square, circle, etc., work out various repeatable patterns of movement in which all travel in and out or around each other.

14

15

Apparatus
1 Travel on the apparatus and surrounding floor deliberately winding in and out of each other.
2 Pairs. Travel on the apparatus and immediately surrounding floor keeping as far apart as possible.
3 Pairs. Travel on the apparatus and surrounding floor **a**) in opposite directions and passing each other **b**) along parallel pathways. (If the apparatus does not allow two gymnasts to work along parallel pathways, one could work on the apparatus and the other on the floor.)
4 Fours. Plan and practise a simple pattern of movement lasting maybe fifteen seconds in which all four travel in and out or around each other on the apparatus and surrounding floor.

5

6

Closing activities
1 Roll, bridge, roll, bridge about the hall.
2 Dive from feet to hands.
3 Practise a favourite movement.

4

5

Support themes
1 Stipulated methods of travelling
2 Shape

Jumping emphasising variety

Flight is extremely exciting and it plays a very important part in gymnastics. It is possible to take off the forehead, neck, shoulder, hands, shins, etc., but of course the easiest method is by taking off and landing on the feet.

In some respects it is easier to jump off apparatus because the additional time in the air allows for various skills to be practised. However, rotation can be set off on take-off and the risk of landing badly is therefore greater when jumping from apparatus, especially in a tucked position. Children should therefore become expert at stretched jumps before they practise tuck jumps from a height.

Mats should be provided when children jump from a height, but care must be taken that the mats do not slip, especially when children are also jumping for distance. Children should be given practise in safe landings at the beginning of every lesson.

Floorwork
There are five basic jumps:

1 from one foot on to the same foot - hopping
2 on and off both feet - bouncing
3 from one foot to the other - leaping
4 from one foot on to two feet
5 from two feet on to one - probably the most difficult.

Apparatus
To start with, simple, low and stable apparatus should be used, such as ropes, hoops, canes, benches, mats, single layers of boxes, agility planks.

It is important that the children be reminded once again of the techniques involved in landing safely and to keep their head high in a tucked jump. They should also be told that the movements between the jumps are as important as the jumps themselves.

Opening activities
1 Travel about the hall from a stretched balance to a roll and continue.
2 Travel about the hall forwards, backwards or sideways.
3 Find interesting methods of taking weight on hands.

4

5

Floorwork
1 Run and jump concentrating on good squashy landings.
2 Run and jump in as many different ways as you can think of.
3 Jump off one foot in as many ways as you can.
4 Jump off two feet in as many ways as you can.
5 Experiment to find how many sorts of jumps there are depending on whether you take off one or two feet and land on one or two feet.
6 Stand and jump as high as possible and land on the take-off spot.
7 Stand and jump as high as possible landing a metre away
   a) forwards b) backwards c) sideways d) diagonally forwards and backwards.
8 Stand and jump a long way a) forwards b) backwards c) sideways.
9 Stand and jump to turn both clockwise and anticlockwise through
   a) 90° b) 180° c) 270°. Land on the take-off spot.
10 Trot four or five paces only to jump as high as possible in the air.
11 Trot four or five paces only to jump a long way.
12 Trot four or five paces only and jump clockwise and anticlockwise through a) 90° b) 180° c) 270°.
13 Practise a variety of running and standing jumps showing a) wide b) narrow c) twisted shapes in the air.

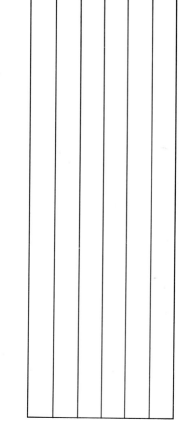

14 Practise a variety of running and standing jumps showing
   a) stretched b) curled (tucked) shapes in the air. (Children should be
   reminded to keep their heads high in order to prevent forwards and
   backwards rotation in the air which is accentuated by tucking.)
15 Trot and jump with a) a hand b) another part as the highest part.
16 Trot and jump with a) a hand b) a hand and a foot c) other
   combinations of parts leading in mid-air.
17 Trot and jump with various body parts stretched to *one* side of the
   body.
18 Join together several different jumps. (Jumps should flow smoothly
   from one to the next. The type of landing will depend on both the
   type of jump which precedes it and the type of jump which
   succeeds it.)
19 Trot and jump high into the air. Tuck at the top of the jump but
   stretch the body immediately after the tuck and before landing.
20 Jump to touch an object above head height, or a mark on the wall,
   etc.

21

22

Apparatus
1 Travel on the floor and apparatus jumping in different ways every
   now and again.
2 Travel in interesting ways on the apparatus and surrounding floor.
   Find places to jump on to the apparatus, over it or off it in
   a) stretched shapes b) curled shapes. (Taking off the feet and
   arriving on the apparatus with hands, or hands and feet, or hands
   and knees, is not really jumping. Nevertheless it is very good
   practice for vaulting as well as good fun and therefore could be
   allowed and sometimes encouraged.)
3 Travel on the floor and apparatus finding places to jump on to the
   apparatus and without a pause off it, along it, *down* off it and *up*
   off it.

4

5

Closing activities
1 Travel about the hall using various rolls.
2 Travel about the hall using hands mainly.
3 Travel about the hall sometimes with legs together and sometimes
   apart.

4

5

Support themes
1 Space in relation to the hall
2 Stopping and stillness

Weight transference

Children have experimented previously (Theme 5) to find the many body parts which can bear their weight.

This theme is concerned with helping children to think in terms of moving or travelling by transferring their weight from one part or parts on to another or other parts. They will also become aware of the different ways in which they can transfer their body weight. The exact skills involved will not be taught in this theme because, since nearly all movement involves transferring body weight, there will be many suitable opportunities to do so later in the scheme of work.

Weight can be transferred using one of four methods:

1　Step-like actions - when the weight is shifted from one or more parts to other non-adjacent parts. The body is in contact with the working surface at all times, e.g. walking, cartwheel, bridge to bridge.
2　Rocking and rolling - when the weight is moved to adjacent parts. (Some people consider it possible to roll or rock on non-adjacent parts if they are placed next to each other.)
3　Flight - when contact with the surface is lost.
4　Sliding - strictly speaking no weight is transferred from body part to body part but only from one location to another.

Children will undoubtedly have experienced movement from each of these categories without realising the fact. They will already be very good at transferring their body weight using feet and to a lesser extent other parts. Much of their time has been spent walking, running, jumping and rolling, and although they need help to perform these actions better, they need even more help to widen their vocabulary of movement and to be conscious of it. Later on they will be able to use this knowledge and experience to make their sequences more interesting and varied.

Floorwork
It might help if pupils say aloud as they are working which parts are taking their weight.

Opening activities
1　Bunny hops with hips high.
2　Run and jump to make *extreme* shapes in the air.
3　Follow-my-leader in threes travelling on feet only.

4

5

Floorwork
1　a) Find many different parts of the body which can be used to support your weight. b) Take up many extreme positions (shapes) using different parts of the body to bear weight.
2　Travel about the hall moving your weight from one part or parts to other parts.
3　Transfer your weight from one part of the body to another and back again by rocking. Repeat using other body parts.
4　Take up a patch balance. Slowly roll your weight on to other patches of the body in a circular direction (e.g. across the shoulders, down one side of the back, across the hips and up the other side to the shoulders).
5　Discover methods of transferring body weight other than by rocking or rolling. How many methods are there? Find a good name to describe each of them.
6　Travel on feet only, using many different step-like actions.
7　Take your weight from two parts to another part or parts a) by placing the new parts down slowly and then transferring weights on to them b) by overbalancing (tipping) under control.

8 Take your weight on your feet, on your hands and then feet
  a) making feet take off and land in the same place **b**) making
  feet land in another place **c**) sideways **d**) forwards.
9 Balance on matching parts and transfer weight to other matching
  parts using step-like actions (e.g. both knees, both feet, both
  elbows, both hands).
10 Step from one part (or parts) to other parts, sometimes with long
   steps and sometimes with short steps. This does not mean feet
   only.)
11 Step from parts of the body to other parts **a**) keeping low to the
   ground **b**) keeping part of the body high in the air.
12 Find several ways of travelling through the air **a**) taking off and
   landing on feet **b**) (if possible) on to or off hands **c**) on to and off
   other parts.
13 Find how many parts of the body on which it is possible to slide.
   Discover how many methods there are of pushing and pulling the
   body into a slide (e.g. pupils can slide as a result of momentum or
   as a result of other parts of the body pushing and pulling).
14 Travel about ten metres using three very different step-like actions.
   (Teachers might prefer to say 'halfway across the hall', etc.)
15 Travel about five metres using three very different rolls.
16 Travel about five metres using three very different types of flight.
17 Travel about ten metres using one method of rolling, one of step-
   like action, one of flight and one of sliding.

18

19

Apparatus
1 Travel on the floor and apparatus using step-like actions.
2 Travel on to, along, off and away from the apparatus using a
  combination of step-like actions and flight.
3 Roll towards, flight on to, step-like action along and a slide away
  from the apparatus. Later on, change the order.
4 Travel on the floor and the apparatus using different sorts of flight.

5

6

Closing activities
1 Travel around the hall curling and stretching.
2 Find several ways of balancing on hands.
3 Bounce around the hall always on two feet but using several
  different methods.

4

5

Support themes
1 Body shape
2 Space in relation to the hall

Theme 19

Rolling

directions

Please read the notes on rocking and rolling (Theme 6).

There is a large difference between 'find several ways of rolling in a forward (backward) direction' and 'do a forward (backward) roll'. The first mentioned task requires children to experiment and find for themselves ways of rolling which are every bit as good in their own right as the formal gymnastic method. In fact, the many answers they find will be extremely valuable both as part of innumerable sequences but also as safety skills in case they fall at some time. It is interesting to note, for example, that parachutists roll over one shoulder when they have landed on both feet, not over two shoulders as in formal gymnastics. Nevertheless, it would be a pity if children were not taught the formal gymnastic rolls at some stage; the great majority are capable of performing them.

Apparatus

A variety of apparatus should be used to allow a range of activity to be pursued. However, each group of apparatus should give children the chance to roll. Low, stable, comfortable and wide equipment, some of it inclining, will help.

Opening activities

1 Run in and out of each other stopping on the teacher's quick word 'stop'.
2 Pairs. Leap-frog over each other.
3 Travel around the hall using hands and/or feet only.

4

5

Floorwork

1 Travel about the hall rocking and rolling in different ways and on different parts of the body.
2 Pairs. One rocks backwards and forwards on his back. His partner gives slight assistance to help him to stand up or crouch. Later try to stand up by yourself from a rock.
3 Roll about the hall experimenting to see how many different shapes you can travel through.
4 Crouch in a curled position. Roll forwards, then sideways and then backwards to finish in a kneeling position. Later, finish by standing up.
5 Perform as in 4 but start and finish in various bridge shapes.
6 Perform as in 4 but start and finish in various balance positions on one body part.
7 Roll in various directions **a**) with the body curled up tight **b**) with the body straight **c**) with legs straight and toes pointed **d**) with the body curled up only mediumly tightly.
8 Stand with feet wide apart. Roll forwards and backwards to stand with feet well apart. (If children tuck their head in before they roll, their spine will curve properly.)
9 Roll, using various methods **a**) forwards **b**) backwards, first over one shoulder only and then over both shoulders.
10 Stand with feet wide apart and roll forwards to finish in a good position without putting hands down first. Find other starting positions from which you can roll without putting hands down first.

11 Perform and improve several different rolls in which you can stand up without using hands.
12 Join two very different rolls together in a smooth flowing way. Repeat and improve and then practise with two other different rolls.
13 Roll about the hall changing direction between rolls.
14 Find several different rolls a) with legs together b) with legs apart.
15 Take up a patch balance and roll away in various directions to another patch balance.
16 Practise rolling in various ways, taking off one, not both feet.

17

18

Apparatus
1 Travel on various parts of your body all over the apparatus and surrounding floor putting different rolls into your work whenever you can.
2 Find various places where you can get on to the apparatus by rolling and then where you can lower a part of your body to the ground and roll away from the apparatus.
3 Roll on the floor to the apparatus, mount it and roll once or twice on it before dismounting and rolling away. Then approach the apparatus from another direction.

4

5

Closing activities
1 Help each other to balance in various ways on the forehead and/or hands.
2 Run, jump, land on one foot and continue running, all in a smooth flowing way.
3 Move around the hall in various ways but concentrating on the legs either being wide apart or absolutely together.

4

5

Support themes
1 Quickly and slowly
2 Direction

Theme 20

Direction

up and down and levels

In addition to moving forwards, sideways and backwards, the body can move up and down. This can be done inside one's own personal space, e.g. from a crouch to a high stretch, or in the general space of the hall, e.g. travel from the floor to a high point on apparatus or jump high into the air.

When children have thought about and have practised moving upwards and downwards, they should consider how long they remain at one *level* and which parts are at any particular level.

In most everyday activities the legs move and remain at low level, the hips at medium and the shoulders at high level. In gymnastics, however, either their relative positions can remain the same but the overall level be raised and lowered, or their relationships can be altered by inverting the body or by working horizontally.

A series of movements can have added interest for the gymnast and onlooker alike if these levels and the time spent at each are varied.

Especially in the initial stages, children should be encouraged to move to positions and levels as extreme as they can manage safely. The results of doing this will be obvious to observers but, more importantly, performers will 'feel' the movement more easily. When they have achieved this understanding, mid-range activities can take their correct place in children's activities. Partners can sometimes be used to coach and encourage performers.

Opening activities
1 Find a variety of ways of rolling with legs straight.
2 Run around the hall, sometimes using steps of even length and sometimes using darting uneven steps.
3 Stand on your hands and kick your legs above your head.

4

5

Floorwork
1 Travel about the hall in various ways, sometimes very close to the ground and sometimes high above it.
2 Crouch close to the ground. Stretch the whole body to reach *as far as possible* a) in front b) to one side c) behind the body. Return to crouch before stretching differently. (At some stage, the teacher should name the body parts to lead the movement.)
3 Balance in a curl mainly on shoulders. Perform as in 1.
4 Start in a *good* bridge shape close to the ground. Stretch one part of the body as high as possible. Return the part to its original position before repeating with another part.
5 Stand with feet apart and hands stretched high to the ceiling. Lower the hands to the floor *in various directions* to take up a good bridge shape. Roll away to another good bridge shape.
6 Walk, trot, hop, stride, jump, etc., about the hall but very close to the ground. Gradually get higher with different parts of the body near the ceiling. Gradually lose height and so on.
7 Find ways of moving on various parts of the body a) with the whole body very close to the ground b) with one part far away from the floor.
8 Take up several upside down (inverted) balances with the whole body near the ground. Stretch a part high to the ceiling, return to another low inverted balance and continue.

9 Take up a position in which one or both feet are higher than the head and travel in that position. Continue in another position.
10 Take up a good patch balance with one part of the body very high. Move to another patch balance close to the ground. Continue.
11 Move around the hall alternating between very high positions and very low positions.
12 Stand about a foot away from the wall. Stretch to touch it as high as possible and remember the place. Use various *standing* jumps to touch the wall even higher.
13 Stand and jump upwards only and stretch fingers as high as possible **a**) directly above **b**) slightly behind **c**) to each side of the head.
14 Trot. Jump with a part of the body as high in the air as possible. Land safely. Repeat with other body parts high.
15 Travel around the hall using jumps, rolls and balances, concentrating on being very close to the ground or having some part as high as possible.
16 Take up a high balance on one leg and change to a low balance on the same leg. Return to the high balance and then repeat with other balances.

17

18

Apparatus
1 Pairs. One holds a hoop or cane in various ways. Partner crosses it at high level and returns at low level.
2 Travel from the floor on to and along the apparatus, gradually gaining height before dropping or jumping off.
3 Travel on the apparatus and the floor around it, sometimes very high in the hall and sometimes very low.
4 Travel on the apparatus sometimes with the whole body close to and sometimes far away from the apparatus.
5 Discover interesting and difficult ways of getting on to the apparatus to take up a high balance before dismounting by using approximately the same method **a**) with a small jump, vault or spring **b**) by rolling, pushing, heaving, sliding, etc.

6

7

Closing activities
1 Roll stylishly **a**) with legs bent **b**) with legs straight.
2 From a balance position on hands and feet, tuck a hand in to roll into a similar balance position a metre away.
3 Find several ways of balancing on hands.

4

5

Support themes
1 Curling and stretching
2 Weight transference

Apparatus work

elementary

Previously, themes have been taught on the floor and the experience gained made more exciting by practising them on the apparatus. For example, simple weight bearing on the floor becomes a balance when performed at a height or on narrow apparatus.

There are some activities, however, which can only be performed on apparatus, e.g. gripping, hanging, heaving, swinging, spinning around bars, climbing, twisting in and out. Children will have performed some of them already in passing; now is the time for them to focus their attention on these activities, not just to become more skilful but more that they should be able to plan for similar activities to be included in their future work.

Since most of every lesson on this theme will be spent on or close to apparatus, teachers might spend longer than normal on teaching carrying and setting up techniques. Skills learned or reinforced will save a great deal of time in future lessons.

Because children enjoy the challenge of apparatus, they tend to get on the apparatus and clamber about it without a great deal of thought and without sufficient planning ahead. Teachers should insist that children sometimes think their activities through before performing them and that now they always attempt to respond to the task that they have been set.

Opening activities

1 Take your weight from feet to hands and bring feet down at another place.
2 Travel around the hall in various ways, sometimes very quickly, sometimes very slowly.
3 Hold hands in twos facing each other. Both travel in the same way about the hall.
4 Travel about the hall sometimes smoothly and sometimes jerkily.
5 Move about the hall sometimes upside down and sometimes upright.

6

7

Apparatus

1 Find several ways of getting on and off the apparatus using arms mainly. When on the apparatus, gain height gradually so that part of you is quite near the ceiling. (Limbs can be used to pull, push, heave, lower, etc.)
2 Find several methods of getting on to and off the apparatus at various places using mainly jumps or some other type of flight. (Flight can very easily be on to hands, knees, stomach, etc., when landing on to apparatus, but on to feet when dismounting.)
3 Get on to, travel about and get off the apparatus using rolling or sliding wherever possible. (Dismounting with a roll is fairly easy off low apparatus or when the body can be lowered gently.)
4 Mount the apparatus, travel on it and dismount from it while hanging from it by different parts or combinations of parts. (For children to be encouraged to hang from the apparatus, the bars should be low or there should be easy access to a nearby escape route. Children can hang from their hands, knees, armpits, elbows, drooping downwards with the bar across their stomach, etc.)

5 Mount the apparatus, travel on it and dismount from it, finding how many parts of the body can be used to grip the apparatus.
6 Take up a balance on the floor, improve it and hold for a few seconds. Move on to the apparatus and try to take up the same balance position in various places on it. Repeat with other balances.
7 Travel on the floor, get on to the apparatus at different places and gain height before dismounting and travelling away from it. Sometimes travel on the apparatus and sometimes suspended from it. (To get on to the apparatus when upside down is not easy.)
8 Travel about the apparatus trying to twist in and out or around parts of it.
9 Travel on the apparatus and the surrounding floor concentrating on being sometimes upside down and sometimes upright.
10 Travel in different ways, sometimes on the floor and sometimes on the apparatus. Every now and again swing on or turn around a suitable piece of apparatus.
11 Travel from the floor on to and off the apparatus within a second or two. Repeat on to and off other parts of the same apparatus or other pieces of apparatus.

12

13

Closing activities
1 Balance, roll and balance around the hall using various balances and rolls.
2 Practise various cartwheel actions using hands and feet.
3 Travel in and out of each other, leaping high into the air and landing resiliently.

4

5

Support themes
1 Personal space
2 Weight transference
3 Stopping and stillness

Use the floor as well as the apparatus

Jumping emphasising technique

Children at this stage of their gymnastic experience should be able to jump in various ways to land safely. This theme will help them to learn more about the techniques involved and will help them to select the sort of jump best suited to their needs at any particular time. Activities which involve landing from a jump and continuing into another movement without a pause are not included in this theme; the landing techniques can be very different and so this work is covered in Theme 39.

It is essential that children are reminded how to make a 'squashy' landing with sufficient give of the hips, knees and ankles to cushion the landing force. A jump from a height will require a deeper landing than a low jump. The head should remain high and children should not topple on to their hands or any other part.

The direction and force of the foot, leg and hip thrust will determine in the main what sort of jump is made. However, the vigour and direction of the arm swing as well as of the chest lift have an important bearing on the sort of jump that follows and they can, for example, impart rotation as well as twisting.

Floorwork
The five basic jumps are:

1 from one foot to the other foot
2 from one foot to the same foot
3 from one foot to two feet
4 from two feet to two feet
5 from two feet to one foot.

Apparatus
It is essential that low stable apparatus is used. Where it is thought necessary to use mats on which to land, ensure that they will not slip. Make sure that pupils are capable of stretched jumps before they attempt tucked jumps.

Opening activities
1 Hold hands in threes and skip together around the hall.
2 Perform cartwheel-type actions using hands and feet.
3 Run sideways in and out of each other.

4

5

Floorwork
1 Run and jump in various ways, concentrating on good landings to stop. Stand up before continuing.
2 Perform as in 1 but with standing jumps.
3 Perform several versions of each of the five basic jumps.
4 Run a few steps and jump *for height*. Which of the five basic jumps is best suited to this? Repeat but with standing jumps.
5 Run and jump *for height* using fast, medium and slow approaches. Which is the most appropriate speed?
6 Run and jump *for distance*. Which of the five basic jumps is best suited to this? Repeat but with standing jumps.
7 Run and jump *for distance* using fast, medium and slow approaches. Which is the most appropriate speed?
8 Run a few steps and jump to make **a**) a wide **b**) a narrow **c**) a tucked (curled) shape in the air. Which of the five basic jumps is best suited to this?
9 Run a few steps and jump to turn through **a**) 90° **b**) 180° **c**) 360° in the air. Which of the five basic jumps is best suited to this?
10 Run, jump and turn in the air. Which speed is most appropriate for a double foot take-off and which for a single foot take-off?

11 Stand and jump a) forwards b) sideways c) backwards, to make
   i) wide ii) narrow iii) tucked (curled) shape in the air. Which of the
   five basic jumps is best suited to this?
12 Stand and jump and turn through a) 90° b) 180° c) 360° in the
   air. Which of the five basic jumps is best suited to this?
13 Stand and jump for a) height b) length. Experiment to discover
   how best to use the legs to ensure the best jump.
14 Stand and jump for a) height b) length. Experiment to discover
   how best to use arms, trunk and chest.
15 Practise jumping to rotate clockwise and anticlockwise a) with
   arms and legs apart in mid-air b) with arms and legs close to the
   body. Which is the better method? How should the arms be used in
   take-off and during flight?
16 Stand and jump sideways off one foot to land on both feet.
   Experiment with how to use the arms and the non-take-off leg to
   assist the jump.
17 Stand and jump sideways off both feet. How far should both legs
   bend before take-off?

18

19

Apparatus
1 Practise standing jumps from various places on the apparatus,
  concentrating on perfect control in flight and landing. Experiment
  when possible with the five basic jumps.
2 Perform as in 1 but run and jump when possible either off the
  apparatus or over it.
3 Jump over moving equipment in groups of two or three, using
  equipment such as ropes, canes, hoops, weighted ropes.
4 Practise standing jumps from various places on the apparatus,
  concentrating on perfect control in mid-air and landing. Use when
  possible the five basic jumps, make shapes and/or turn in mid-air.

5

6

Closing activities
1 Pairs. One takes up a bridge position and the other travels under,
  over and round him.
2 Balance on hands for several seconds. Repeat using another
  method.
3 Roll around the hall in sideways and backwards directions.

4

5

Support themes
1 Shapes in the air
2 Limbs together and apart

Body parts leading a movement

This theme will extend the children's gymnastic repertoire by making them aware of the various parts of the body which can be used to lead movements. The front, side and back of the body are normally used to lead everyday movements, but the head, feet, a foot, knees, a knee, elbows, an elbow, hands, bottom, chest among many others frequently lead in gymnastic movements.

In most activities of any duration, one part or area of the body leads for a period of time and then the other areas take over the lead. However, in some actions, e.g. rolls, the parts leading the movement are continuously changing. It is best, however, to concentrate in the early stages of this theme on a certain part leading a movement throughout.

At first, children will tend to move the leading part in the easiest and most obvious direction - they will need help in thinking of alternatives. To take one simple example, from a standing position with legs astride, the most obvious way of moving is to stretch both hands forwards, sideways or upwards. Children should be helped to think of other less obvious actions; they could make one hand or an elbow lead their movement; both hands could stretch in different directions but one could become the more dominant; their hands could travel backwards, or between their feet or to the side of one of their feet. Children should very soon use these actions to lead them into a new movement, e.g. a jump, flight on to hands, rolls, twists, pendulum-type actions, curls, stretches, overbalancing on to hands.

The children should be encouraged, when they are more competent, to make their body shape clearly defined.

Apparatus
Pupils are still relatively inexperienced and this theme can lead gymnasts into activities they have not experienced before. They should normally be expected to respond to the task given to them by the teacher, but they should be allowed a certain flexibility of response for this will provide a safety factor.

Opening activities
1 Jump on the spot making up your own rhythm.
2 Run and jump high into the air. How many ways can you stretch in mid-air?
3 Slow bunny jumps with 'high tails'.

4

5

Floorwork
1 Travel concentrating on using different parts of the body to lead the movement.
2 Choose a part of your body and find how many ways you can travel with that part leading the movement. Choose another part.
3 Take up various balance positions. Discover how many and which parts can lead a stretch away from the body and then how many and which parts can lead a curl back towards the body.
4 Travel on all fours, stomach facing downwards. Discover how many parts or areas of the body can be used to lead the movement.
5 Travel as in 2, but with stomach facing upwards.
6 Move around the hall on feet only, sometimes shuffling, striding, gliding, moving stealthily, moving boldly, swooping, rushing, etc. Which parts lead most naturally for each type of movement? Repeat the movements with other parts leading.
7 Perform several *standing* jumps from each of the five categories (Theme 22). Discover how many and which parts of the body can lead the movement.

8 Perform several *running* jumps with different body parts leading.
9 Perform four standing jumps, each being led by a different body part.
10 Find as many ways as possible of travelling with the following parts leading: **a**) toes **b**) heels **c**) hands **d**) elbows **e**) head **f**) shoulders **g**) knees **h**) from head down the back of the body to the heels.
11 Take up a bridge shape on two feet and one hand. Use the free hand to lead the body into a roll into another similar bridge shape.
12 Balance on various parts of the body. Find out how many other parts can lead you into a twist.
13 Take up a bridge shape on one foot and two hands, the free leg leading a twist and roll into another similar bridge shape.
14 From a variety of bridge shapes experiment with different parts of the body (shoulder, elbow, knees, etc.) leading the body into rolls and a finishing position three or four metres away.
15 Discover several jumps and practise one or two in particular, in which the movement is started by **a**) a swing of the 'free' leg **b**) a swing of both arms **c**) a swing of the upper body.
16 Travel several metres by curling and stretching with different parts leading.

17

18

Apparatus
1 Arrive on and, where safe, dismount from the apparatus **a**) hands first **b**) feet first **c**) with other parts leading.
2 Travel around the apparatus twisting and turning, curling and stretching as appropriate with different parts of the body leading the way.
3 Travel to the apparatus with one part leading, on to and along the apparatus with another part leading, and away from it with a third part leading.
4 Spring on to the apparatus with the front of the body leading, travel along it with the head leading and leave it with the feet leading.

5

6

Closing activities
1 Walk lightly around the hall showing good style.
2 Lie on the ground, firstly in a tense manner and then in a completely relaxed manner.
3 Roll in and out of each other in various ways but without touching.

4

5

Support theme
Shape

Pathways

direct and flexible

Children will realise by now that the body can move in many directions, e.g. forwards, backwards, sideways. They will also know that their limbs can follow tracks of pathways within their own personal space, e.g. towards or away from their body centre or around the periphery.

The manner in which a person travels is the most important part of gymnastics. The theme covered here deals with the pathway that the body follows on the floor in a two-dimensional way; the third dimension, that of level, was considered in Theme 20.

Pathways are placed in two categories: direct and indirect (sometimes called 'flexible'). Direct pathways (those which involve travelling in a straight line) are normally the more functional in character, especially when speed of action is involved. Indirect pathways can give an interesting, individual, even artistic, character to the work.

Examples of indirect pathways include: circles, spirals, rectangles, triangles, arcs, heart shapes, clover-leaf, letters of the alphabet, numerals. Some take the body from a starting place to a destination some distance away, while others return the body to its original starting position. Some patterns are large, some small and some repeat themselves - the options are immense.

Theme 40 is also devoted to pathways and teachers are asked to read it before starting.

Teachers are reminded that pathways are not the same as direction (Theme 12). Both will be combined in Theme 40. It is suggested that pathways are taught with no mention being made of direction.

Floorwork

Children should experiment with pathways using the simplest form of travel, i.e. on feet only. When they have grasped the idea of pathways making patterns on the floor, their teacher might well stipulate other modes of travel, e.g. on hands and feet; from feet to hands; on other named parts; various rolls; curls and stretches; balance, roll, balance; jump, roll, jump, roll; bridge shapes; cartwheel-type actions; jumps and turns.

Apparatus

Apparatus gives a wonderful opportunity to include changes of level but in order not to confuse the children, it is better not to use that element in this theme but to consider just the two-dimensional approach as has been done in the floorwork.

Simple, low apparatus should be used for the first lesson or lessons. It should be arranged so as to allow for a variety of pathways. Apparatus which encourages many different methods of travel should be introduced once the children begin to work along imaginative pathways.

Children should be reminded that if they employ a variety of pathways when using the apparatus they will not have to queue, especially if they vary their starting and finishing positions.

Opening activities
1 Jump rhythmically on the spot to the teacher's handclap.
2 Practise a favourite movement.
3 Practise cartwheel-type actions around the hall.

4

5

Floorwork
1 Travel about the hall in various ways concentrating on the pathway you trace on the floor. Find several different types of pathway and give each a suitable name.
2 Travel with different parts of your body leading the movement, sometimes following a curving pathway, sometimes an angular and sometimes a straight pathway.
3 Choose a destination five metres away and travel to it in a straight line by **a)** trotting **b)** using hands and feet only **c)** rolling **d)** various jumps **e)** bridge and roll to another bridge **f)** some other method.
4 Travel, using different methods, to a destination ten metres away following various zigzag paths.

5 Travel, using various methods, to a destination ten metres away. Follow various indirect pathways all of which involve straight lines joined by angles.

6 Travel freely around the hall following angular pathways.

7 Travel, using various methods, to a destination ten metres away. Use single curving pathways to get there.

8 Travel, using various methods, to a destination ten metres away. Follow 'S' pathways of varying sizes.

9 Travel, using various methods, to a destination ten metres away combining a curved and a straight pathway.

10 Travel on different parts of the body following a circular pathway.

11 Travel on different parts of the body and return to the starting point following a) curving b) straight angular pathways.

12 Travel with different body parts leading, tracing on the floor a chosen letter of the alphabet.

13 Travel with different body parts leading, tracing on the floor a chosen numeral.

14 Travel, sometimes upside down and sometimes upright, to a destination ten metres away following a direct pathway. Return to the starting point following a smooth curve.

15 Work in a square pattern travelling in different ways along each side.

16

17

Apparatus

1 Stand in a space five metres away from your destination on the apparatus. Travel to it following the direct pathway, turn round and return to the starting position, again in a straight line.

2 Travel as in 1 but follow angular, straight-lined pathways.

3 From a starting point five metres away from the apparatus, travel to your destination five metres on the other side of it. Follow a variety of a) angular b) curving c) straight pathways.

4 Imagine a line on the ground about three metres away from the outside of your piece of apparatus. Using various starting points on this line, approach the apparatus and balance on it before changing direction, dismounting and moving to another point on the imaginary line. Use various direct and indirect pathways.

5

6

Closing activities

1 Balance, twist and roll into another balance. Continue.

2 Find several balances with your legs high in the air.

3 Stand and jump in various directions showing different shapes.

4

5

Support theme

Various methods of weight transference

Partner work

obstacles to be negotiated without contact

It is important that children learn to work co-operatively with each other. Handling apparatus and working together in groups on apparatus have already provided plenty of opportunities for this. This theme is the first of several designed to teach children to work together in pairs or small groups.

Children do not necessarily have to be paired with others of equal ability and size. Teachers might prefer boys and girls to work together in each partnership, or to give children a completely free choice. They might feel it wise to ensure that the less popular children are not left on their own and that new partnerships are formed at least every lesson. In any case, they should ensure that each child in a partnership gets an equal experience of leadership.

This theme will help children to observe each other's movements and plan their own in such a way that both harmonise in an interesting and demanding way. They should become aware of each other's strengths, weaknesses and intended actions.

They will soon learn that negotiating people can be much more fun than negotiating apparatus, especially when both are moving at the same time.

Floorwork
When children work in pairs, a certain amount of discussion will be necessary, but this should be quiet and at a minimum. It will be usual for one partner either to take up a position or to perform a sequence and for the other to observe it; they can then work together. When they become more skilled, they will be able to work together without an observation period for they will have the experience to adapt their own movement to accommodate that of their partner.

Partners should normally change from being an obstacle to being negotiator when it best suits their work, but sometimes when requested to do so by their teacher. Children should be encouraged to use variety when first answering a task, but should develop one or two answers to a very high, repeatable quality.

The exact mode of travel has not normally been stipulated though the teacher could direct it by stipulating, for example, the parts of the body which should take their weight or lead the movement, the speed, the direction, the pathway, etc., of the movement.

'Squashy' landings should follow those activities which involve a jump.

Apparatus
By now, children ought to be very confident on the apparatus. However, negotiating each other will impose new difficulties and therefore apparatus should be very carefully chosen. With nervous children it might be wise not to expect them to work on all apparatus but to let them choose where they work.

It should be possible for several pairs to be working at the same time on a group of apparatus if the floor is used as well as the apparatus.

When negotiating each other both partners need not be on top of the apparatus; one could be suspended from it, or be on the floor.

Opening activities
1 Trot around the hall performing various jumps off one foot.
2 Travel around the hall using stretches, curls and rolls, without the feet touching the ground.
3 Run in twos, trying to 'lose' your partner.

4

5

Floorwork
1 Find as many ways as you can of crossing over or going past your partner without touching him.
2 A lies on the floor in various shapes and B travels *over* him a) with a jump b) on hands and feet c) using another method.
3 A makes various bridge shapes and B travels *underneath* him a) in a stretched position b) in a curled position.
4 A makes various bridge shapes and B travels *over* him a) with a jump b) using hands and feet.

5 A makes various wide balance shapes and B travels *around* him with a) stomach uppermost b) back uppermost.
6 A adopts various bridge shapes and B winds in and out and through.
7 Half the class adopts various bridge shapes and the other half travels freely under, over or around them.
8 A travels using various bridge shapes, B negotiates him.
9 A rolls around the hall, sometimes in a curled position and sometimes in a stretched position. B travels over A a) with a jump b) using hands and feet.
10 A rolls *towards* B who travels over him. Both continue to a finishing position.
11 A travels five metres to a destination first in a bridge shape and then by balance, roll, balance. B observes and then negotiates A when he repeats his sequence. B can negotiate A from head-on or from the side, or can overtake him.
12 A and B start to travel fairly close to each other and in roughly the same direction. First A negotiates B, then B negotiates A. Carry on until they arrive at their destination.
13 The whole class travel using jump, rolls and bridge shapes. When two children meet, they carefully pass each other in the most appropriate way.
14 Perform as in **13** but using individual ways of travelling.

15

16

Apparatus
1 A takes up a position on the apparatus and B negotiates him in the most appropriate way.
2 A and B approach the apparatus from opposite directions and negotiate each other before continuing to their planned finishing location.
3 A and B move on the floor and apparatus quite freely and negotiate each other as appropriate when they meet.
4 The whole class travels freely on floor and apparatus, paying particular attention to negotiate each other in a variety of ways.

5

6

Closing activities
1 Find various ways of balancing on both hands.
2 Run around the hall changing the rhythm about every ten seconds.
3 Leap as high as possible into the air and turn before landing.

4

5

Support themes
1 Weight bearing
2 Weight transference

Balancing

Theme 5 on weight bearing should be referred to.

When planning work for her class, it can be quite tricky for a teacher to know just how difficult it will be for the children to change from weight bearing to balancing, though her individual children will be in no doubt at all.

Probably most four-year-olds can stand on the floor quite easily and for them that is weight bearing. Ask them to stand on a fairly high box and for many of them that activity will become a balance.

Most eleven-year-olds can stand on a high box quite easily, even on a high horizontal ladder, but ask them to stand on a high narrow beam or on a skateboard and probably weight bearing will have changed to balancing for many of them. All balancing has a wobble factor, probably a risk factor as well, but above all it is individual to each one of us.

Balancing can be made more difficult by:

1 reducing the area of the base (standing on toes with feet together)
2 raising the centre of gravity in relation to the base (standing up high)
3 raising the working surface (standing on a high box)
4 reducing the area of the working surface (standing on high beam)
5 working on a moving surface (standing on a trapeze bar)
6 inverting the body (balancing on hands)
and several other methods.

Because balances are difficult to hold, it is important that children first practise them in circumstances in which falling out of them is not risky. They should then be given practice in what to do when they overbalance. In most cases a gymnast can put another part down for support and then try to balance again. Alternatively, he could move away on to another part; this is one reason why children should practise moving from one balance to another. Standing on a high piece of apparatus is very different, however. A gymnast must try to keep his balance but must know exactly how far he can go and still be safe. At some point he must grab something for support, or, more likely, he must jump down to the floor - hence the importance of floorwork 22 and apparatus work 2.

Lastly, because balancing is by its nature static, children should be asked to hold balances for a few seconds only and surround balances with plenty of movement.

Apparatus
Care should be taken that the apparatus is stable and is raised in height and reduced in area gradually. Instructions should be sufficiently embracing for nervous children to be able to find a satisfactory answer just as easily as the more adventurous.

The decision as to whether to support youngsters when balancing on apparatus is a difficult one and must be left to each teacher. However, my view is that if the child requires support then he should normally attempt the task under easier conditions.

Opening activities
1 Run and jump to make various shapes in the air.
2 In twos, one travels in various ways on his feet, the partner follows and copies.
3 Run, jump and roll around the hall.

4

5

Floorwork
1 Move about the hall stopping every few seconds to balance in a different way on different parts of the body.
2 Find and practise a variety of balances on a) three parts b) two parts c) one part.
3 Find pairs of parts on which to balance, e.g. forearms, hands, knees, toes, heels.
4 Find various parts of the upper body on which to balance.
5 Find a way to balance on the hands, if possible with the bottom or legs high.

6 Find a three-point balance. Slowly 'walk' the position of one of these points to make the balance more difficult.

7 Stand, slowly lean forwards until out of balance and then quickly move a foot forwards to 'save' yourself. Repeat in other directions.

8 Perform as in 7 but from other easy and safe balance positions.

9 Balance on two hands and a foot, stomach downwards. Slowly take one hand away and use it to help balance the body. Repeat but with stomach upwards. Find other bridge shapes on three parts, slowly take one part away and balance.

10 Stand on both feet; a) slowly take one foot off the ground to stretch it out backwards and high; find a variety of good positions using the hands and chest to keep balance b) repeat with leg going sideways and forwards, c) repeat but stand on other leg.

11 Take up other two-point balances and do as in 9.

12 Find a big patch balance and then make it more difficult by reducing the area. Repeat with other patch balances.

13 Balance on your bottom with arms grasped around the knees. Gradually loosen the grip by the hands and stretch the legs outwards near the ground and then gradually raise them in the air. Counter-balance as necessary with the rest of the body and arms. Repeat with other patch balances.

14 Balance on one foot. Experiment by stretching arms upwards, sideways, forwards and backwards, to discover the effect of various arm positions.

15 Find a variety of balances on one or two parts. Move other parts of the body fairly slowly at first, trying to keep in balance.

16 Take up a balance position and then roll into another.

17 Take up a balance position and twist into another.

18 Take up a balance position and turn into another.

19 Trot and jump to land in a good balance position on a) two feet b) one foot.

20 Take up a balance position. Discover how far you can lean or stretch forwards, sideways or backwards, to lightly touch the ground without losing balance. Repeat in other starting positions.

21 Find a balance and overbalance into a roll.

22 Stand in a good balance position. Gradually lean forwards. When balance is about to be lost, jump forwards to balance again on your feet. Repeat in other directions.

23

24

Apparatus

1 Move on the floor and apparatus, stopping every few seconds to take up a new balance. (If children begin to overbalance, it is important that they should learn to jump off the apparatus to land safely on their feet, rather than be tempted to fight for their balance for too long and risk landing badly.)

2 Stand on your apparatus, near to the ground. Slowly and slightly overbalance to the front, jump the feet forwards to land safely on the ground. Repeat sideways and backwards if confident.

3 Move about your apparatus in good style and balance first on three parts, then two parts and finally one part.

4 Move purposely about the apparatus and balance where possible on the upper half of the body.
5 Take up a balance position and either roll, twist or turn into another balance position with a different part high.
6 Stand on the floor with hands on the apparatus. Push off the legs to balance on the apparatus in a variety of positions on different parts.

7

8

Closing activities
1 In twos, one takes up a high bridge shape, the other travels through in good style. Alternate.
2 Travel keeping close to the ground.

3

4

Support themes
1 Shape
2 Parts high
3 Travelling between balances.

Theme 27

Sequences

short and simple

A sequence is quite simply the joining together of several movements in such a way that they form a pleasing whole. Because very few movements are performed in isolation, children have already performed countless sequences, usually, however, without conscious thought. The intention here is to make children aware of what a gymnastic sequence is and to help them to construct one successfully.

Too long or difficult sequences should be avoided as these would mean the children would probably produce poor or unclear sequences. The first sequence could join two simple short actions, or could be composed of one short main activity with a short preparation to this action and a short recovery from it.

There are two main ways (and several in between) in which children can be taught to perform a sequence.

The first is the main one to be used in this theme because it is the most applicable to novice gymnasts although it should also be used on occasion with the more experienced; the teacher sets a fairly broad task and the children perform the consequent sequence with very little prior thought and planning - they just let it happen as long as it answers the task set. They will find that one movement flows quite naturally into the next and frequently the sequence is quite different from anything they would have composed in their mind beforehand. They will be asked to perform quite short sequences - probably lasting five or ten seconds. They will then be expected to repeat the sequence several times improving its individual components and cutting out any 'stuttering' or untidy joining movements. They will also be expected to show definite starting and finishing positions to each sequence.

The second method is to ask gymnasts to plan their total sequence before actually performing it. This requires a wide movement experience and a vivid imagination and is therefore more applicable to very competent gymnasts. More will be said about this method in the relevant sequence themes.

The teacher might like the children to work in twos on occasion. They should observe each other and offer constructive advice.

Opening activities

1 Travel using various methods a) forwards b) backwards
   c) sideways.
2 In pairs, travel in zigzags negotiating each other without touching each other.
3 Travel around the hall in many different bridge shapes and rolls.

4

5

Floorwork

1 Move about the hall changing very smoothly from one method of travelling to the next.
2 Decide on a good bridge position. Find several short movements which take you into this position and several to take you out of it. Choose the best sequence into and out of the bridge position. Repeat with other positions.
3 Proceed as in 2 but using a jump from one foot on to the other as a main activity.
4 Perform as in 2 but with a roll.
5 Perform as in 2 but with a difficult balance.
6 Join two different jumps together smoothly. Concentrate on good starting and finishing positions.
7 Join two different bridge shapes together with a twist.
8 Link five different slow giant steps so that each flows into the next
   a) forwards only b) some forwards and some sideways c) some forwards, sideways and backwards.

9 Link five different standing jumps off and on to both feet so that each flows into the next **a**) forwards only **b**) some forwards and some sideways **c**) some forwards, sideways and backwards.
10 Link a variety of jumps and steps into a flowing sequence.
11 Practise a variety of **a**) curled **b**) stretched **c**) various direction rolls. Link three or four together into a pleasing sequence.
12 Stand, sink and roll away in various ways to a good finishing position.
13 Walk in various directions and various manners to sink and roll to a good finishing position.
14 From an exciting starting position roll away three or four metres to a good balance.
15 Balance, roll, balance, roll and balance.
16 Run, jump and land in a good balance position. Hold for two seconds and roll to another balance position.
17 Move from a stretched position to a curled position and continue.
18 Jump, land, roll, jump, land, roll and balance.
19 Travel about five metres taking the weight from feet to hands to feet to hands and finish in a balance position on feet.

20

21

Apparatus
1 Travel along the apparatus without prior planning, concentrating on smoothness at all times.
2 Take up a wide shape on or suspended from the apparatus. Travel to a different balance and repeat to a finishing balance.
3 Roll two metres on the floor, mount the apparatus, move along it using hands and feet only, move away from the apparatus to a finishing position two metres away. (The sequence should be short, i.e. consist of only three or four components.)
4 Travel smoothly on the floor and apparatus alternating between curled and stretched positions.
5 Plan ahead and then perform a sequence on to, along and off the apparatus, concentrating on smoothness at all times.

6

7

Closing activities
1 Find several ways of balancing on hands only.
2 In pairs, follow my leader.
3 Leap frog over your partner.

4

5

Support themes
1 Pathways
2 Shape

Time

quickly and slowly

All actions require time for their completion and there are many ways in which this can be used. The most obvious way is either to spend a long time or a short time over completing an action and this will dictate how slowly or quickly one works. Alternatively, a gymnast can spend more time on performing the beginning of an action and less on the remainder of it and this will mean that acceleration takes place. Likewise, actions can be given a rhythmical quality by the way time is used in their completion.

Most movement is not isolated but is part of a sequence of activity. Each element of a sequence can use time differently so the variety is immense.

In most cases, activities are best performed at a certain speed, or with acceleration, or with deceleration, or at an even tempo, etc. Nevertheless, each individual gymnast must also bring his own influence to bear and his exact intention, his ability, his physique, etc., will all help to decide the best way for him to perform an activity.

Children will already be very adept at, for example, running quickly or slowly but will not have thought consciously about the time factor. This theme should make them aware of the use of time in gymnastic movement and in later themes they will experiment with acceleration and deceleration, sustained and sudden movement, rhythm, etc.

Floorwork
At first, children should concentrate on performing actions either extremely quickly or extremely slowly; they will be able to do this if the actions are fairly short and simple rather than long and complicated. A terse quick word of instruction like 'go' will often result in a terse quick action.

Later on, children should experiment with speed in order to be able to select that which answers their requirement best.

Apparatus
It will be easiest to start off with simple, single pieces of apparatus. When sequences are required, it might be easier to use the floor as well as the apparatus, rather than to join several pieces of apparatus together. This will encourage youngsters to repeat their work, aiming for high quality, rather than 'wandering around' on the apparatus.

Opening activities
1 Run and jump, concentrating on good landings.
2 Travel variously around the hall **a)** forwards **b)** backwards **c)** sideways.
3 Travel variously around the hall first with feet, and then with head leading.

4

5

Floorwork
1 Travel about the hall in various ways, sometimes very quickly and sometimes very slowly.
2 Stand in a position of readiness. On a signal from the teacher stretch the arms to their full extent in various directions, and on another signal, bend them again **a)** very slowly **b)** extremely quickly. Later on, move without a signal from the teacher.
3 Perform as in 2, but from other starting positions, e.g. a three-point balance.
4 Perform as in 2, but lift and lower various parts of the body.
5 Perform as in 2, but curl and stretch the whole body, not just a small part of it.
6 Stand in an alert position, lunge in a stated direction (forward, sideways, backwards) **a)** in a controlled fairly slow manner **b)** very quickly and urgently.

7 Perform a short sequence of jumps, some very slow and some very quick.
8 Walk about four paces **a)** very slowly **b)** very quickly.
9 Walk around the hall alternating between very slow and very quick actions.
10 Run about four paces **a)** very slowly **b)** very quickly.
11 Run, alternating between sudden bursts of great speed and sudden changes to slow controlled running.
12 Travel sideways from feet to hands to feet **a)** very slowly **b)** very quickly.
13 Roll around the hall, sometimes very slowly and sometimes quickly.
14 Perform as in **12** but using other methods of travel, e.g. hopping, travelling on four points.
15 Run six or seven paces before changing direction through 90° **a)** slowly **b)** quickly. Discover the best speed.
16 Compose an interesting sequence lasting about ten seconds which shows contrasts in speed. Repeat in order to attain high quality work.
17 Compose an interesting sequence lasting about ten seconds which starts and finishes slowly but has a very quick middle. Repeat in order to attain high quality work.

18

19

Apparatus
1 (Mats only) Travel on the floor on hands and feet, sometimes very quickly and sometimes very slowly. When you come to a mat, roll across it either very quickly or very slowly.
2 Find ways of crossing your apparatus either very quickly or very slowly.
3 Travel on the apparatus and surrounding floor alternating between very quick and very slow movements.

4

5

Closing activities
1 In pairs, follow my leader travelling in ways stipulated by the teacher.
2 Travel around the hall with either the feet or the hands as the highest parts for most of the time.
3 Travel around the hall following various curved pathways.

Support themes
1 Weight transference
2 Moments of stillness
3 Pathways

Partner work

pathways

Floorwork

Activities **1** to **3** are designed to remind the class of what is meant by pathways. Some will need to spend longer on this aspect and teachers might find it helpful to reread the contents and teaching points in Theme 24.

The emphasis should be on the pathways used although the mode of travel is obviously important. The teacher should stress that the pathways and the action should be simple and short enough for the partner to recognise and copy successfully.

It is a matter of co-operation not competition. Time must be given for quiet discussion, comment and for children to coach each other. Children should plan their work fairly well before performing it, not 'as they go along'. They should be able to repeat what they have done. It is important that their actions have good distinct starting and finishing positions.

Partners should take it in turn to lead.

Apparatus

There could be a certain risk in asking young or inexperienced gymnasts to copy each other's activities on apparatus. To start with, great emphasis should be put on the need for the leading children only to perform actions which they know their partners can copy and for the 'following' children only to attempt to copy activities which they know they can perform safely.

They should be reminded that the pathway of their activities is the theme of the lessons, not the activities themselves.

Opening activities

1 Practise a favourite activity.
2 Travel around the hall sometimes taking all weight on hands.
3 Run around the hall jumping to turn in the air.

4

5

Floorwork

1 Travel *individually* about the hall along pathways of straight lines linked by angles **a)** on feet only **b)** on hands and feet mainly **c)** using other methods stipulated by the teacher **d)** using other methods chosen by the individual.
2 Perform as in **1** but travelling along a variety of curving pathways **a)** on feet only **b)** on hands and feet mainly **c)** using other methods stipulated by the teacher **d)** using other methods chosen by the individual.
3 Plan and perform individually a pathway which will visit three places in the hall and return the performer to his starting position within about twenty seconds **a)** on feet only **b)** on hands and feet mainly **c)** using other methods stipulated by the teacher **d)** using other methods chosen by the individual.
4 Pairs. One person trots around the hall concentrating on a varied but obvious pathway which his partner is capable of following. The partner follows about a metre behind concentrating on copying the pathway exactly.
5 Pairs. Perform as in **4**, but travelling **a)** using a variety of foot only actions **b)** using hands and feet only **c)** using jumps and rolls **d)** using other methods as selected by the teacher **e)** using methods of children's own choice.

6 Pairs. One person trots to a finishing point about ten metres away following an imaginative but relatively uncomplicated pathway. He repeats this exactly. The partner observes and then copies exactly.

7 Pairs. Perform as in 6, but travelling a) using a variety of foot only actions b) using hands and feet only c) using jumps and rolls d) using methods of children's own choice.

8 Pairs. Both discuss and agree a simple method or methods of travel and a pathway to reach a destination ten metres away in a straight line. Both practise this so that they can perform simultaneously, one behind the other.

9 Pairs. Perform as in 8, but following a pathway which will return them to their starting point.

10 Pairs. Perform as in 8, but following a pathway, e.g. circle, triangle, square, figure, figure of 8 when each partner can start at opposite sides of the figure.

11 Pairs. Discuss and agree simple methods of travelling along pathways which involve meeting each other and then parting to return to own starting point.

12

13

Apparatus

1 Pairs. Both cross and recross simultaneously a single piece of apparatus and the space immediately surrounding it while interfering as little as possible with the other's progress.

2 Pairs. One travels on, around and under a single piece of apparatus following a) a curving pathway b) an angular pathway c) various types of pathways; the partner follows a metre or so behind.

3 Pairs. Perform as in 2 but moving freely around the hall from one piece of apparatus to another.

4 Pairs. One travels towards the apparatus, then along, over or under it, then away from it a) on feet only b) on hands and feet c) by other simple methods. Partner observes and then copies.

5

6

Closing activities

1 Move around the hall from patch balance to point balance to patch balance and so on.

2 Move around the hall alternating between normal speed and slow motion.

3 Balance in several ways on hands only.

4

5

Support themes

1 Quickly and slowly

2 Shapes

Rolling

variety and joining together

Children should now be very good at rolling safely. This lesson will widen their experience and will serve as a lead up to a later theme when they will jump in various ways, then land and roll.

Rolls are often used as linking movements in sequences as well as being interesting components in their own right.

In this theme, many children will be rolling, sometimes very quickly in a confined space. They must be aware of what other children are doing and be prepared to adjust their actions in order to prevent collisions.

Opening activities
1 Dive bunny jumps around the hall.
2 Pairs. Run, jump over partner and turn in the air to land facing him.
3 Standing long jumps around the hall a) off two feet b) off one foot.

4

5

Floorwork
1 Stand, sink to the ground and roll away in various directions to stand and continue.
2 Take up a good, unusual starting position balanced on one or two feet. Twist, sink and roll away in various directions to jump in the air, land on one or two feet and continue.
3 Take up various contrasting starting positions. Roll away in various directions but bring both feet directly over the shoulders when upside down.
4 Perform several similar rolls in the same direction, sometimes very quickly and sometimes very slowly. Change the type of roll and repeat.
5 Perform as in 4 but either start slowly and accelerate, or start quickly and decelerate.
6 Link several rolls together without the hands touching the ground once. Repeat with other rolls.
7 Sit on the ground with legs apart and straight. Roll in various directions to a good finishing position, trying to keep legs straight all the time.
8 Link several rolls together, sometimes similar and sometimes dissimilar, trying to keep the legs straight and toes pointed whenever possible.
9 Perform as in 7 but grasp the legs near the ankles for as long as possible during the roll.
10 Perform a sequence containing four different rolls with a change of direction and/or speed.

11 Take up a crouch position. Place hands on floor/mat and roll forwards to stand up. Repeat and when competent go through the air slightly before placing hands on floor/mat. Gradually increase the time spent in flight, but never let the head touch the floor or mat. (Dive forward rolls – when a gymnast takes off one or both feet, flies through the air, and then absorbs his momentum with his hands before continuing into a roll to stand up – are extremely exciting. Only competent gymnasts (those who can roll safely over both shoulders without their head ever touching the ground) should be set this task. Even good gymnasts should not be pressurised, but only encouraged to travel through the air. In any case, they should only travel a short distance.)

12 Balance on forehead while also being supported on one or two other parts. Tuck the head in and roll away in various directions.

13 Pairs. Both perform several rolls along zigzagging paths. Take it in turn when both meet to roll under or over each other.

14 Experiment to find a very good sequence which involves in the most appropriate order several very different rolls, flight and moments of stillness.

15 Find several different rolls in which a twist can be performed during the roll.

16 Pairs. Work side by side and perform identical sequences involving three different sorts of roll.

17 Pairs. Develop a continuous sequence in which each takes it in turn to jump over the other and roll.

18

19

Apparatus

1 Travel on the apparatus and the surrounding floor using contrasting rolls as well as movements on hands and feet.

2 Devise and practise several different sequences lasting about fifteen seconds containing in any order two different rolls, two different balances, two leaps and other joining movements.

3 Move on the apparatus and surrounding floor in exciting ways including trying to roll uphill or downhill, on to, along, or off the apparatus.

4

5

Closing activities

1 Run and perform several split jumps.

2 Run and jump to touch toes with hands in various ways.

3 Practise wheeling actions around the hall.

4

5

Support themes

1 Pathways

2 Limbs together and apart

3 Shape

Twisting

Twisting happens either when one end of the body or a limb rotates around its length while the other end is held still, or when both ends are rotated in opposite directions, as when wringing out a towel by hand. By contrast, turning takes place when the whole body rotates in the same direction.

In gymnastics the most valuable twisting takes place in the spine. This mobility is a great asset for everyday activities, but it also opens up a whole new range of gymnastic movement. Children should experience and recognise a feeling of real torsion in their bodies; taking up twisted shapes is probably the quickest way of doing this. However, the main thrust of the lessons should be on the action of twisting as a part of functional movement, not on

holding twisted shapes.

Twisting can also take place while children curl or stretch. This corkscrew action is very difficult but very satisfying to perform.

Floorwork
When twisting in mid-air, children will learn that before jumping it helps to twist the body in the opposite direction to that intended in mid-air.

Apparatus
Because twisting often results in a change of pathway, the apparatus should be sited to allow this to happen.

Opening activities
1 Run, jump and land in many different ways.
2 Travel by jumping from feet to land on hands.
3 Follow-my-leader performing a variety of jumps.

4

5

Floorwork
1 Find as many ways as you can of twisting all of your body or part of it.
2 Make twisted shapes while resting on different parts of the body.
3 Stand with feet comfortably apart. Twist the rest of the body clockwise and anticlockwise as far as possible, hold for a few seconds and return to the standing position.
4 Perform as in 2 but from other starting positions, some of them inverted.
5 Take up a curled position. Stretch out the body and twist it at the same time. Hold the end position and then return to the curled position by untwisting. Repeat from other curled positions.
6 Adopt a bridge shape on feet and hands, a) keep the feet fixed and walk the hands round the feet as far as possible and then return b) vice versa.
7 Balance on hands with legs high. Twist and lower the legs down to a new place each time.
8 Balance on one part. Twist the rest of your body or parts of it in as many ways as you can. Repeat in balances on other single parts or patches of your body.
9 Stand and jump in the air to take up a very twisted shape. Land in the starting position.
10 Run and jump to take up a twisted shape in mid-air.

11 Stand and jump high but twist on take-off to turn vigorously in mid-air.
12 Perform as in **10** but use a slow run-up first.
13 Take weight on both feet and one hand. Use the other hand to lead the body into a twist followed by a roll into another bridge shape. Continue.
14 Balance on three parts, twist to balance on another three parts.
15 Transfer the weight from feet to hands, twist the body before taking weight on feet again.
16 Roll, twist, roll, twist, etc.
17 Plan and then perform a short sequence involving three twisting actions.

18

19

Apparatus
1 Move about the apparatus and floor frequently twisting the whole body or part of it.
2 Find various ways of mounting and dismounting the apparatus by twisting, normally while in continuous contact with the apparatus but sometimes using flight.
3 Take up a balanced shape while on or suspended from the apparatus. Use a part of the body to lead it into a twist and thence to another balanced shape.
4 Travel about the apparatus finding different ways of twisting round horizontal, vertical and sloping pieces of apparatus.

5

6

Closing activities
1 Balance, roll, balance, roll and continue.
2 Join together into a sequence three different jumps.
3 Move using hands and feet only.

4

5

Support themes
1 Pathways
2 Sequences which involve twisting
3 Body parts leading

Body parts lifted high

Children will be very proficient at travelling or holding positions with their head being the highest part of their body - they are doing so for most of their waking day. The object of this theme is to give them practice in moving with many other parts of their body being lifted high, either while their body is supported on other parts or while it is lifted in flight.

The basic experience can probably best be given by using held positions but such work can become extremely boring. Children should soon be expected to travel through or in these positions.

For children to experience real stretch, teachers should often ask for extreme positions and not accept in-between positions.

Floorwork

With some classes it is of value to ask the children to give a running commentary on which part is the highest at any moment.

By this stage children should be learning to plan their work before they perform it. To assist children in this and to check their ability, teachers should sometimes ask them to describe exactly what they intend doing before they start performing.

Apparatus

The apparatus should be chosen to suit exactly the work to be carried out so that it is not so high that the children cannot concentrate on the task in hand.

Opening activities

1 In pairs, travel all over the hall negotiating each other without contact.
2 Travel from feet to hands to feet following a direct pathway.
3 Travel in various ways but alternating between very wide and very narrow shapes.

4

5

Floorwork

1 Travel about the hall in various ways, concentrating on changing the body part which is highest at any one time.
2 Take your weight on both feet and experiment to find how many different parts and groups of parts can become the highest part of the body.
3 Stand on one foot and perform as in 1 above.
4 Take up a variety of bridge shapes on two or three points so that your feet are extremely high. Repeat so that **a**) a foot **b**) stomach **c**) a hand **d**) an elbow **e**) a knee is extremely high.
5 Take up a variety of patch balances with parts named by the teacher as the highest part.
6 Travel slowly on feet only so that the highest part of the body changes regularly.
7 Travel from one bridge shape to another, concentrating on changing the body part which is held as high as possible.
8 Link four bridge positions into a sequence so that various body parts are held high. Repeat and improve.
9 Travel from a balance on shoulders through a good sitting position to a balance on one leg, concentrating on having three different parts very high at different times.

10 Travel about the hall sometimes very quickly and sometimes slowly. Concentrate on changing regularly the highest part of your body.

11 Find various ways of travelling holding a part named by the teacher as the highest part. Construct a sequence, improve and repeat.

12 Travel from feet to hands to feet, concentrating on having the following part extremely high at one time in the movement **a)** foot or feet **b)** hand or hands **c)** the head **d)** the hips.

13 Run and jump high in the air to take up a good position with **a)** a hand **b)** two hands **c)** an elbow **d)** the head as the highest part. (Children should be warned not to allow unintentional rotation to take place.)

14 Perform a standing jump with **a)** the non-jumping foot becoming higher than the rest of the leg **b)** the non-jumping foot becoming higher than your chest **c)** one knee becoming as high as possible but not necessarily the highest part of the body. (Children should be warned not to allow unintentional rotation to take place.)

15 Perform a five metre long sequence containing a roll, a curl and a balance. Say aloud which part is the highest at any time.

16

17

Apparatus

1 Travel on the apparatus and the floor changing frequently the part of the body which is held as high as it could possibly be.

2 Find several methods of mounting and dismounting from the apparatus so that various parts of the body are the highest part at different times. (This can, of course, include flight.)

3 Plan and perform a short sequence involving travel on floor, moving on to, along and off the apparatus and travelling away from it. Plan for different parts to be the highest part at various times.

4

5

Closing activities

1 Travel taking weight on various parts but always moving backwards.

2 Travel using various cartwheel-type actions.

3 Travel by joining various balances and twists.

4

5

Support themes

1 Direct and indirect pathways

2 Direction

Partner work

contrasting and matching movements

In Theme 29, children were required to observe each other's actions and to copy them with reasonable accuracy, particularly as far as the pathway was concerned. By now, they will have become far more skilful and will be experienced enough to be able to copy safely another person's actions as well as pathways.

In addition to extending the children's repertoire of movement by adding to it the best and most interesting activities of other gymnasts, their observation will be trained and in turn quite severely tested. If they can analyse their partner's action and think of a contrasting action, or if they can observe their partner's movement and then copy it exactly, this is proof that their observation and analysis have been accurate. Furthermore, learning to observe accurately other gymnasts' work will help them to do the same for their own.

If, however, a few children are still finding it difficult to observe accurately a partner's work, it might help them if they are required to give a quiet running commentary.

Sometimes, children will be expected to copy their partner's work immediately, sometimes after the whole sequence has been performed once or twice, and sometimes after a short discussion.

Once again, this theme requires co-operation, not competition, and children should be told to select those activities which they believe their partner can perform.

Partnerships should consist normally of youngsters of comparable ability and for this theme they will tend to work one behind the other because this is the simplest way. Later on, some children might choose to work side by side and should be allowed to do so. However, this is to be covered in Theme 42, as is working face to face. Working back to back is very difficult and will not be taught until Theme 50.

Apparatus
It is essential that:

1 the originator be told to choose movements which his partner is capable of imitating
2 the partner be told not to attempt movements of which he is not confident.

Opening activities
1 Transfer weight from feet to hands to feet a) on the spot b) while travelling.
2 Pairs. Cross over each other by a) a jump b) putting hands on the floor at some time.
3 Practise a variety of high leaps, sometimes using both feet, sometimes just one.

4

5

Floorwork
1 One takes up a variety of shapes on a) one foot b) both feet
   c) various combinations of three points d) various patches
   e) various difficult but good balance positions. Partner stands behind and copies immediately.
2 Proceed as in 1 but with the leader performing a) simple curls and stretches b) simple rolls c) transferring weight from one part to another.
3 One takes up a shape and his partner observes and then takes up a contrasting (very different) shape. Repeat with other extreme shapes, then balances, then simple rolls and lastly simple transferences of weight from one part to another.
4 One performs a special jump. Partner observes and then copies as exactly as possible. Repeat with other jumps. Continue in the same way with various rolls, then turns in mid-air, then curls and stretches.

5 One travels around the hall, his partner following two metres behind and trying to copy exactly **a**) on feet only **b**) on feet only with changes of speed **c**) rolling **d**) transferring body weight from part to part **e**) jumping **f**) using bunny hops, cartwheels, crawling, giant steps, skips, etc.

6 One performs and repeats a short interesting sequence on feet only but involving a change of speed. Partner observes from behind and then repeats exactly.

7 Proceed as in **5** but include a change of direction as well.

8 One performs a sequence involving a run, jump, twist and landing in a good balance position. Partner observes and copies.

9 One performs a ten second sequence of his own choice. Partner observes, then copies.

10 Both discuss and practise a short sequence that they can perform simultaneously, one behind the other.

11 Proceed as in **9** but use components as suggested by the teacher.

12 One performs a single action. Partner repeats it and adds another component. First repeats both components and adds another and so on until a sequence with six component actions is formed.

13

14

Apparatus

1 One demonstrates body shapes on or suspended from the apparatus. Partner observes and copies exactly. Repeat with other point and patch balances.

2 Proceed as in **1** but use jumps on to, along and off the apparatus.

3 Proceed as in **1** but use various methods and locations for mounting and dismounting from the apparatus.

4 Follow-my-leader on the apparatus using very simple methods of travelling.

5 One demonstrates a short sequence involving travelling five metres to, along and away from the apparatus. Partner observes and copies.

6

7

Closing activities

1 Balance on hands with feet high.

2 Pairs. Find interesting and safe ways of helping each other to balance.

3 Join together two high jumps and one long jump in any order.

4

5

Support theme
Space (personal and general)

Theme 34

Turning and spinning

It is important that teachers realise all the ways in which gymnasts can turn and spin so that they can ensure that their children have experience of them all. Most older children can understand the theory involved, and if this is covered in the classroom before the gymnastic lesson, much better work will result.

Turning occurs when the body rotates around any one of its three main axes:

1 its long axis from head to toe as when standing and turning to face another direction or when rolling in the stretched position
2 its side-to-side axis across the hips or shoulders as in a forward or backward roll
3 its front-to-back axis from stomach to spine as in a cartwheel; this is probably the most difficult.

Spinning occurs when the body turns around a point in contact with the floor or apparatus, and momentum continues the rotation (a spinning top). When rotation has been started, its speed can be increased by shortening the lever or decreased by lengthening the lever; i.e. if a gymnast spins on one toe with his arms stretched out wide, he will spin more slowly than if he puts his arms close to his body.

Apparatus
Tasks practised on the floor normally become more exciting when performed on to, on or off the apparatus. There are some turning and spinning activities which can only be practised using apparatus, e.g. around vertical, horizontal or angular ropes, bars and platforms. Swinging when suspended from hands or legs is also a form of turning, albeit through only a few degrees. Care should be taken not to use apparatus which is too high.

Opening activities
1 Pairs. Travel towards, negotiate without contact and travel away from each other.
2 Travel, twisting out of one bridge shape into another.
3 Run and jump, making different shapes in the air.

4

5

Floorwork
A *Around the long axis of the body*
1 Imagine that you have a line through your body from your head to your toes. Find several ways of turning your body around that line when stationary and while moving.
2 Stand and with a series of small movements of the feet rotate the body clockwise and anticlockwise a) slowly b) quickly. Discover the effect of either having arms out sideways or by the side.
3 Perform as in 2 but with the head and shoulders leading.
4 Jump high into the air to turn round as far as possible before landing a) clockwise b) anticlockwise. Find the best way to prepare for the jump and the effect of wide and narrow shapes.
5 Take up a long horizontal bridge shape or lie on your side and find several ways of turning around the long axis of your body.
6 Practise in a short sequence several ways of turning around your long axis a) sometimes with your body curled and sometimes straight b) with different parts of the body causing the rotation.
B *Spinning*
7 Stand and spin, in both directions, on the ball of one foot. How many turns can be made with arms outstretched or by the side?

78

8 Perform as in 7 but change shape during the spin.

9 Find other parts of the body on which you can spin.

   C *Around the side-to-side axis*

10 Imagine that you have a line through your body from one hip to the other. Find several ways of turning your body around that line.

11 Turn around the side-to-side axis in a forward and backward direction from **a**) the crouch position **b**) a balance on shoulders **c**) sitting **d**) kneeling **e**) with a small dive from feet to land on hands.

   D *Around the front-to-back axis*

12 Imagine that you have a line from the front of your stomach to your backbone (spine). Find how you can turn your body around it.

13 Crouch close to the floor. Roll sideways across your shoulders to finish in a crouch position **a**) towards the left **b**) towards the right.

14 Sit on the floor with legs astride. Roll sideways across your shoulders to finish in a sitting position **a**) towards the left **b**) towards the right.

15 From a crouch position, place the hands to one side and take the body weight on to them with bottom high.

16 Cartwheels to left and right.

   E *Various*

17 Compose and practise a sequence which involves rotation around each of the main axes.

18

19

Apparatus

1 Travel on the floor, the apparatus and through the air performing whenever possible movements in which you turn or spin around your long axis. (Children will probably need to be reminded sometimes to have other parts of the body than their head as the highest part, and that they can be suspended from the apparatus as well as being just on top of it.)

2 Travel on the floor and the apparatus performing whenever possible movements in which you turn around your side-to-side axis and in which you turn around your front-to-back axis.

3 Make up and carry through a sequence in which you turn around each of the three axes of your body.

4

5

Closing activities

1 Travel around the hall in pairs, one copying accurately the movements of the other.

2 Travel on hands and feet, covering the whole floor-space of the hall.

3 Travel, showing extremes of stretched or curled positions.

4

5

Support theme
Matching work with a partner

Pathways

selecting compatible pathways and activities

The previous themes (24, 29) involving pathways for gymnasts working singly or in pairs should be referred to.

The intention here is to widen the children's experience and to make them more critical and selective in the pathways they follow for various types of activity and vice versa. Of course, each needs to be in sympathy with the other. If, for example, the performer intends to run in a straight line to a destination and then either to return along the same line or to travel away at an obtuse angle, he must slow down before he arrives at the destination and he must then overbalance in the new direction; the greater the angle through which the gymnast turns, the greater becomes the need to slow down. Likewise, the faster the gymnast travels, the greater the need becomes for a very strong bend of a leg followed by a push in the required direction. Similarly, if a gymnast intends following a smoothly curving pathway, it would be unwise to travel by

a series of large leaps - smaller turning leaps would be better.

It is probably easiest in the first lessons to stipulate the pathway which children should follow and ask them to practise and select suitable methods of travel. Later on the teacher can stipulate the method of travel and ask children to find suitable pathways.

The last stage is when individual children construct and perfect sequences which involve a variety of pathways and activities of their own choice, or when two children co-operate to produce combined sequences. When performing the work in this theme there are great advantages in working in pairs, one observing and helping the other.

Children will sometimes change direction (i.e. that area of the body which leads a movement) at the same time as they change their pathway. This will be covered specifically in Theme 40 and it is suggested that the gymnasts' attention is not drawn to this aspect until the later theme.

Opening activities

1 Pairs. Dodge and mark while travelling on hands and feet.
2 Pairs. One travels from bridge shape to bridge shape, the other negotiates.
3 Travel by linking balances and rolls.

4

5

Floorwork

1 Use many different methods to travel first along a direct pathway and later along various curving pathways to a destination five metres away.
2 Find suitable methods of travelling while following **a)** a triangular pathway **b)** a square pathway **c)** an irregular angular pathway.
3 Travel **a)** in a straight line **b)** along a zigzag to a destination ten metres away by jumping and turning in mid-air through **a)** 45° **b)** 90° **c)** 180°, landing and rolling.
4 Link balances, twists and rolls; travel along a semi-circular pathway to a destination.
5 Use first jumps, then step-like actions and lastly any favourite method to travel around a circular pathway.
6 Travel on hands and feet **a)** following a clover-leaf pathway **b)** using other unusual pathways.
7 Practise several and then select the best pathway to follow when travelling to a given destination using methods involving **a)** a series of bounding jumps **b)** a series of different rolls **c)** a run, jump and landing in a balanced position **d)** twists and turns.

8 Decide on a sequence which involves travelling ten metres. Practise it at a very high speed, then at slow motion, then with acceleration and lastly with deceleration. Discover the best speed. Repeat with another sequence.

9 Practise several ten second sequences following a circular pathway and several changes of level. Practise the best for high quality.

10 Pairs. Discuss, experiment and then perfect a sequence to be performed simultaneously involving appropriate movements along a pathway stipulated by the teacher. Repeat with other sequences.

11 Travel freely around the hall using either very smooth or very jerky movements and following various direct and indirect pathways. Later on practise a short sequence involving particularly suitable combinations.

12

13

Apparatus

1 Travel around the hall, visiting and moving across or along pieces of apparatus. First follow indirect pathways on the floor and direct pathways on the apparatus, and then vice versa.

2 Travel on and around apparatus using it as a) the central point of a clover-leaf pathway b) the apex of a triangle.

3 Travel on the floor and the apparatus following angular pathways.

4 Travel from one piece of apparatus to another following curving pathways. Try to change level gradually.

5

6

Closing activities

1 Pairs. Find interesting ways to help each other to balance.

2 Pairs. Find interesting balances on each other.

3 Find various balances on one body part.

4

5

Support themes

1 Partner work – matching movements

2 Space in the hall

Sequences

longer and more complicated

The teacher and pupils will be reminded of the sequence work already carried out by referring to Theme 27.

There are times when children should be encouraged to work within the limits set but at the same time to allow their movements to develop as they happen; movements can flow quite naturally and without prior planning from one to the next, but with inexperienced gymnasts this does not often result in contrasting activities, exciting action or unusual work.

During this theme children should spend about half their time performing spontaneous sequences and half on planning sequences fairly accurately before embarking on them. Of course, it will be necessary for the gymnast to experiment to find several sequences which answer the task set, to select the best, to alter and adjust this one where necessary and lastly to practise it for perfection.

Gymnasts should first select compatible components which best answer the task set. These components might have similar characteristics, e.g. the same speed, level, symmetry, or they might have contrasting characteristics. More experienced gymnasts can sometimes make their sequences more stimulating for themselves and observers alike by including contrasts of direction, pathway, effort, shape, etc. They might also include inverted positions or movements, pauses, extreme balances, but again these will have to be well planned before the gymnast embarks on his sequence. Pupils will need the help and encouragement of the teacher if they are to be capable of such fine planning. They should also be reminded of the need for every sequence to have a good starting and finishing position.

Because it is normally easier to recognise good or poor movement in what others do than in what one does oneself, it is helpful sometimes to work in twos. Children should be encouraged to give and to receive constructive and helpful comment. They must remember, however, that the performer's intentions are the important ones and should not be altered to accommodate those of the observer.

Opening activities

1 Jump on the spot rhythmically, changing the rhythm every so often.
2 Move on hands and feet, changing frequently the body part nearest the ceiling.
3 Pairs. Hold hands and find ways of travelling sometimes on feet and sometimes on other parts.

4

5

Floorwork

1 Travel around the hall, sometimes on the floor and sometimes in the air. Concentrate on flowing actions and eliminate 'stutters'.
2 Select two contrasting balance shapes. Find three different methods of moving from one to the other while travelling two metres.
3 Select three contrasting balance shapes. Find several methods, and then practise the best, of moving from one to the next while travelling five or six metres.
4 Join, in any order, a patch balance, a spin, a roll, a jump and a bridge shape to form a good sequence.
5 Travel freely around the hall extremely slowly, changing the body part which leads the movements. Concentrate on very smooth flowing actions.
6 Plan and practise a sequence involving six different held shapes joined by twists and rolls. Later, move *through* the shapes.
7 Experiment, then select and practise a sequence lasting about twenty seconds, the first actions to be performed very quickly, the next slowly and deliberately, and the last quickly once again.

8 Travel around the hall on feet only using very different actions and directions, sometimes in a staccato fashion and sometimes smoothly.

9 Compose several sequences involving in any order, sideways leaps, turns, rolls and balances. Select one sequence and practise.

10 Compose several fifteen second sequences involving in any order, balances, spins and twists. Select one and practise.

11 Travel from feet to hands to feet with a twist; follow this with a jump roll and balance.

12 In pairs. One demonstrates three times a favourite fifteen second sequence. Partner observes, comments and suggests improvements. Performer alters and improves his sequence.

13 Join three identical jumps into a pleasing sequence by inserting two different linking movements.

14 Move around the hall, sometimes forwards, backwards and sideways, alternating between having the head and then another body part highest.

15 Practise a sequence in which you start and finish with the same movement. Change to another sequence.

16

17

Apparatus work
1 Travel freely on the floor and apparatus, concentrating on flowing actions and eliminating stuttering actions, then compose a suitable, interesting sequence.

2 Prepare and refine a sequence which consists of holding contrasting shapes on the apparatus and the floor and joining them with suitable movements. Repeat but travelling through the shapes without holding them.

3 Prepare and refine a sequence composed mainly of jumps, rolls and held positions on the apparatus and surrounding floor.

4 Compose several fifteen second sequences on the apparatus and surrounding floor consisting of travelling on hands and feet, on feet only and through the air.

5

6

Closing activities
1 Try to push up into or walk over into a crab position.
2 Pairs. Practise wheelbarrows.
3 Balance on hands.

4

5

Support themes
1 Partner work matching movements
2 Pathways

Theme 37

Partner work

assisting balance and supporting each other's weight

For this theme to be taught successfully it is essential that children realise the importance of ensuring each other's safety. It can be used as a means of helping children to adopt a responsible and caring attitude towards each other, but until this exists it would not be wise to use apparatus.

The work in this theme is mainly concerned with supporting part or all of a partner's weight. Actively lifting another person will be dealt with in Theme 47 and, because that involves very important lifting techniques, teachers are advised not to include it in their work at this stage.

The easiest and safest way of learning to control another person's weight is to help him hold a difficult balance and this is the first category of work covered in this theme.

The second category of work, which involves partners using each other to hold combined balances that each could not hold separately, requires that each puts his trust in the other. There is little chance of an accident if the combined balances fail, but the work is quite demanding and very enjoyable.

A counter-balance is one in which partners lean against each other and maintain a combined balance.

Counter-tension is when they grip each other and lean outwards away from each other.

The third category of work in this theme involves one person providing a platform on which his partner can work.

Apparatus
Apparatus should be low, wide and stable.

The teacher should not stipulate too exactly what each person must do.

It is even more important when using apparatus that the children behave sensibly and with a caring attitude.

Opening activities
1 Travel around the hall on hands and feet, sometimes the feet being the highest part.
2 Pairs. Follow my leader.
3 Pairs. Travel about the hall on different body parts. One tries to lose his partner by sudden changes of speed.

4

5

Floorwork
1 One describes a simple balance position to his partner and then attempts to adopt it. Partner assists him to hold the balance by steadying him. Gradually choose more difficult balances.
2 Stand facing each other sideways on or back to back and find several ways in which to lean against each other and remain in balance. Try to move slowly in unison while remaining in balance.
3 Take up a variety of positions fairly close to each other. Find ways of gripping each other and leaning away from each other into a combined balance.
4 Compose sequences in which both travel five metres towards each other, grip each other, then lean away from each other, pull up to the vertical, let go and move to a good finishing position.
5 Find several ways of leaning against your partner at high level, then gradually lowering to near floor level before returning to high level.
6 One takes up a strong position. The other finds several balances in which part of his weight is on the floor and the rest on his partner.

7 A takes up a strong position on all fours. B finds several ways of balancing with all his weight taken on A.
8 Discuss and then practise several ways of one person getting on to his partner and being carried around the hall.
9 Find several ways of travelling in twos around the hall with one person's weight being taken partially by his partner and partially on the floor.
10 Discuss and then practise several movements in which A climbs on to B and then shifts his weight or changes his shape before lowering himself to the ground.
11 Find several ways in which one takes up a strong position at a low level. Partner approaches and crosses him from one side to the other by a) putting some weight on him b) putting all his weight on him.
12 Compose and practise several sequences involving starting five metres apart, both travelling to each other, one supporting his partner's weight and both travelling away to a finishing position five metres apart.
13 Find several exciting ways in which two people can provide a platform on which the third person can move and balance.
14 Find several interesting ways in which one person can assist two others to hold difficult balances.

15

16

Apparatus
1 Find various ways in which one person's weight is distributed between a piece of low stable apparatus and his partner.
2 Find various ways in which one person can dismount from apparatus with some of his weight being taken by his partner.
3 Find suitable places on low, stable apparatus where one person can safely support all or most of his partner's weight.
4 Find various methods of travelling on the floor and apparatus where one person takes all or most of his partner's weight.

5

6

Closing activities
1 Run and jump showing different shapes in the air.
2 Move around the hall frequently taking weight on hands.
3 Roll into a jump, continue around the hall in a variety of ways.

4

5

Support themes
1 Lifting parts high
2 Shapes

Shape

symmetry and asymmetry

The conscious decision by a gymnast to use symmetry or asymmetry as a component of his movement can add great variety and quality. Children should now be able to understand and use the concepts involved and it is suggested that only one or two periods are spent on introducing the concept. Children can continue on to other themes and return to this one every now and again in order to enrich their work.

To appreciate the meaning of symmetrical movement, children should imagine a line running from the top of their head and down their spine to the floor. If each side of this line moves identically then the movement will be symmetrical; if each does not, then the movement will be asymmetrical. The use of phrases like 'lopsided and balanced', 'even and uneven', 'both sides doing the same or not doing the same' might help children to understand the meaning of 'symmetry' and 'asymmetry'.

Teachers will realise that children can recognise such a quality in someone else's work better than in their own. It might also be helpful to discuss the subject in the classroom and to use diagrams, etc.

Practically, symmetry and asymmetry can be most easily understood by taking up static positions, but once the idea has been completely appreciated, attempts should be made to move and travel through or in these shapes.

Children will soon realise that most natural movements like walking, running, jumping, twisting and turning are performed asymmetrically. Many vaulting and agility activities as practised in formal gymnastics tend to contain symmetrical movements and as such require great body control. Teachers might therefore think it best to spend longer on symmetrical than on asymmetrical actions.

Opening activities
1 Travel round the hall joining jumps and rolls.
2 Travel taking weight on hands frequently.
3 Move about the hall in such a way that the whole body is used and becomes warm.

4

5

Floorwork
1 Stand on both feet and move the trunk, head and arms to take up a series of symmetrical and asymmetrical shapes.
2 Perform as in 1 but move through shapes to produce sequences.
3 Balance on shoulders and elbows. Move a) trunk and legs b) the whole body including shoulders and arms to take up various symmetrical and asymmetrical shapes.
4 Balance as in 3 but travel through shapes.
5 a) Balance symmetrically on various patches or pairs of points to find several shapes where the whole body is symmetrical.
b) Balance asymmetrically on various patches or points to find several shapes where the whole body is asymmetrical.
6 Balance as in 5 but move through shapes.
7 Find various bridge shapes when the whole body is a) symmetrical b) asymmetrical.
8 Travel, alternating between held symmetrical and asymmetrical bridge or balance shapes.
9 Travel as in 8 but move through the symmetrical and asymmetrical bridges.

10 Spin on various parts of the body **a**) symmetrically
   b) asymmetrically.
11 Jump variously to make symmetrical and asymmetrical shapes in
   the air.
12 Perform sequences involving various symmetrical and asymmetrical
   jumps, take-offs and landings.
13 Roll in various directions **a**) symmetrically **b**) asymmetrically.
14 Travel about the hall in various ways but symmetrically for about
   ten seconds and then asymmetrically for about ten seconds.
   Continue.
15 Travel on feet only, using them symmetrically for about ten seconds
   and then asymmetrically for about ten seconds.
16 Travel in various ways using the hands symmetrically for about ten
   seconds and then asymmetrically for about ten seconds.
17 Jump, land and roll either forwards or backwards into a balance
   position **a**) symmetrically **b**) asymmetrically **c**) alternating
   between both.
18 Compose a twenty second sequence showing contrast of
   symmetrical and asymmetrical movements.
19 Pairs. Discuss and then take up combined balances which are
   symmetrical; change them to asymmetrical balances.

20

21

Apparatus
 1 Travel freely on the floor and apparatus, alternating between
   symmetrical shapes or movements and asymmetrical shapes or
   movements.
 2 Find several places and methods of mounting and dismounting the
   apparatus **a**) symmetrically **b**) asymmetrically.
 3 Choose and then practise a sequence of movements lasting about
   twenty seconds and travelling five metres on to, along and off
   apparatus, showing contrasts in symmetrical and asymmetrical
   movements and positions.

 4

 5

Closing activities
 1 Try to walk on hands.
 2 Find ways of balancing on your partner.
 3 Balance, twist, roll to balance.

 4

 5

Support themes
 1 Lifting parts high
 2 Level

Jumping, landing and rolling

Rolling has been covered in Themes 6, 19 and 30 while jumping has been covered in Themes 9, 17 and 22. Teachers are asked to remind themselves of what was done at those times.

The ability to land and flow into various rolls is essential for gymnasts so that they can produce interesting sequences of work and also correct any slightly faulty landing by absorbing their body weight and momentum safely into a roll.

The variety of combinations is immense and children should experience a great number of them. However, as an increasingly important part of their work from about now on, they should be expected to make selections of their best responses to tasks and then to hone them for extremely high quality gymnastics.

Floorwork
Mats which will not slip should be provided for children to roll on, not necessarily to land on, especially if rolling is to play a large part in several consecutive lessons.

Apparatus
It is particularly important that children are absolutely competent at jumping and landing from apparatus before they are asked to add on a roll.

Apparatus should not be too high and should be completely stable. Inclined apparatus will allow children to select the height from which they jump.

A variety of starting and finishing points should be provided.

Opening activities
1 Cat spring about the hall.
2 Move about the hall using curls, stretches, twists and turns.
3 Move sideways on hands and feet.

4

5

Floorwork
1 Practise a variety of jumps **a)** forwards **b)** sideways **c)** backwards **d)** turning.
2 Practise various rolls, going forwards, backwards, sideways and over a shoulder.
3 Run and jump showing a variety of shapes in the air and landing in **a)** a 'squashy' fashion **b)** a 'more bouncy' fashion.
4 Stand, sink slowly to the ground and roll away in various ways and directions to a finishing position. Sometimes twist as you sink.
5 Walk forwards, then backwards and lastly sideways to sink and roll away to a finishing position.
6 Run slowly forwards, then backwards and lastly sideways to sink and roll away to a finishing position.
7 Jump on the spot, gradually increasing the height, and land to sink and roll away **a)** forwards **b)** backwards **c)** sideways.
8 Jump on the spot to land on one foot, immediately followed by the other foot before sinking and rolling away.
9 Stand and jump a short distance **a)** forwards **b)** backwards **c)** sideways. Land and roll away first in the direction of travel and later in other directions.
10 Run and jump high into the air. Land and roll away first in the direction of travel and later in other directions.

11 Run and jump turning in mid-air to land facing the take-off spot. First continue into a roll in the direction of travel (backwards) and then towards the take-off point (forwards) and lastly sideways.

12 Pairs. One takes up a bridge shape on the floor. The other runs and jumps over him, sometimes turning in the air and sometimes not. On landing he rolls either over or under his partner.

13 Practise and improve several sequences which include a jump forwards, a jump sideways and a jump backwards, each being followed by a roll.

14

15

Apparatus

1 Find various places on the apparatus from which to jump
a) forwards b) backwards c) sideways, or hang by hands and drop on to feet. When landings are perfect, add on a roll in the direction of travel.

2 Practise as in 1, but where possible take a few steps along the apparatus before jumping forwards, landing and rolling.

3 Find various places from which to jump forwards but turn in mid-air to land and roll in the direction of travel.

4 Travel on the floor and apparatus, sometimes jumping over, on to or off the apparatus to land and roll. Where possible hang by the hands from the apparatus, drop, land and roll.

5

6

Closing activities

1 Travel around the hall frequently taking weight on hands with legs high.

2 Leapfrog in pairs.

3 Follow-my-leader in pairs.

4

5

Support themes

1 Partner work – matching movements

2 Symmetry and asymmetry

Theme 40

Directions and pathways

This theme is designed to help gymnasts to discover the various ways in which directions and pathways can be combined in order that later they can select those combinations which will suit their needs best.

The following will be remembered from Themes 12, 20, 24 and 35.

Direction is concerned with which area of the body predominantly faces the direction of travel, i.e. one can travel forwards, backwards, sideways, head first, feet first, etc.

Pathway is concerned with the track that the gymnast follows on the floor, on the apparatus or through the air. A gymnast can travel to his destination along a direct pathway, i.e. in a straight line. Alternatively he can travel along any one of innumerable indirect (flexible) pathways. Some indirect pathways will consist predominantly or solely of straight lines, e.g. triangular, rectangular, zigzag pathways, while some will consist predominantly or solely of curving lines, e.g. circular, semi-circular, spiral, eliptical pathways.

To simplify matters, emphasis in this theme will be placed on pathways in the horizontal plane.

There are four basic ways in which pathways and directions can be combined:

1   The gymnast can travel along a constant pathway with the same part of the body leading throughout.
2   He can travel along a constant pathway, changing the body part which leads the movement.
3   He can change the pathway with the same part of the body leading throughout.

4   He can change the pathway and the part of the body which leads the movement.

Children will be asked to practise each of these while travelling in various ways and it is hoped that the experience will help them further in making their work interesting, varied and good.

Floorwork

To start with it pays to ask children to walk back to their starting position each time. When they have 'got the idea' they can turn round and work back to their starting position or another destination, thereby saving time.

Foot-only methods include running, bounding, striding, hopping, the five methods of jumping, Cossack walking, crouch jumping, skipping and countless methods without a name.

Hand and foot methods will include crouch jumps, crab walks, bunny hops, cartwheel-type actions, handstand fall over into crab and many 'unnamable' actions.

Other methods of travel can include transference of weight from and to named body parts, balance, roll balance, jumps, twisting, turning, curling and stretching.

Apparatus

Travelling from the floor to apparatus and on different parts of the apparatus also brings in another type of pathway, i.e. change of levels, and therefore children cannot in fact travel in a straight line. This complicating aspect should be disregarded for the time being.

Opening activities

1 Jump, turn in the air, land and add a movement.
2 In pairs, negotiate each other while travelling around the hall.
3 Practise a favourite sequence.

4

5

Floorwork

1 Travel freely about the hall following a whole variety of pathways, forwards, sideways or backwards.
2 Use various foot-only methods to travel *in a straight line* to a destination ten metres away **a)** forwards **b)** backwards **c)** sideways all the way **d)** changing direction part way.
3 Repeat as in 2 above but travelling on hands and feet.
4 Repeat as in 2 above but using in any order jumps, rolls and transference of weight from hands to feet.

5 Travel variously on feet only to a destination ten metres away, following a zigzag pathway **a)** first facing forwards for the whole journey, then backwards and finally sideways **b)** changing direction.

6 Travel as in **5 a)** and **5 b)** but on hands and feet.

7 Travel as in **5 a)** and **5 b)** but use other methods of travelling.

8 Travel along a curving pathway to a destination ten metres away using runs, jumps and landings **a)** first facing forwards for the whole journey, then sideways and lastly backwards **b)** changing direction (not pathway) during the journey.

9 Travel to a destination ten metres away following various indirect pathways and using various modes of travel **a)** first facing forwards all the way then sideways and lastly backwards **b)** changing direction as appropriate.

10 Travel along a variety of pathways which return you to your departure point, sometimes travelling forwards, sometimes sideways and sometimes backwards. Use several modes of travel.

11 Travel sideways about the hall, concentrating on following a variety of pathways and travelling in many different ways. Repeat travelling backwards.

12 Face and remain facing a chosen place in the hall. Travel to it following various pathways **a)** on feet only **b)** transferring weight to and from various body parts.

13 Plan and then perform a short sequence which involves travelling in various ways in various directions along interesting pathways.

14

15

Apparatus

1 Travel freely about the floor and the apparatus, concentrating on following a whole variety of pathways, sometimes forwards, sometimes backwards and sometimes sideways.

2 Stand three metres away from the apparatus and decide on a destination three metres the other side of it. Travel to this destination following various pathways, sometimes forwards, sometimes backwards and sometimes sideways.

3 Face a chosen destination on another piece of apparatus. Travel to it facing it all the time but following various pathways.

4

5

Closing activities

1 Practise balancing on hands with feet high.

2 Practise cartwheel-type actions.

3 Balance, roll, balance, roll and so on.

4

5

Support themes

1 Stopping and stillness

2 Partner work – matching movements

Shape

style

Teachers are asked to read the previous themes on shape (15 and 38).

The emphasis in this theme is on the shape of the body as it is moving rather than when it is still. Body awareness is essential of course to a gymnast because he must know the position of body parts in relation to each other even when in unusual positions. Children should therefore be made more aware of their body shape in motion both while in contact with the ground and while in flight. They will practise some actions where their body shape changes during the movement and others where their body shape remains fairly constant, e.g. cartwheels.

While developing a reasonable kinaesthetic awareness, a gymnast will come to realise the need for holding or passing through good shapes and will become aware of what these are. In formal gymnastics, this is resolved fairly easily because the gymnastic associations decide in large measure what is or is not good style. In educational gymnastics the situation is nowhere near as clear cut because there are no rules and regulations, no rights and wrongs. Movements can be performed equally well using a whole variety of body shapes. Much will depend on the task set, but much also on the exact intention of the gymnast. It follows, therefore, that before the teacher or a partner can advise a gymnast on how to improve his style, he must find out exactly what the gymnast is trying to achieve and only then can he suggest that his back should be straight, arched or curled; whether his head should turn to the side, to the front, upwards or downwards; how much his knees should bend; whether his toes should be pointed or cocked up, etc.

However, a few general points can be made about good style as far as shape is concerned: all shapes should feel good and look good; they should be efficient and help to answer the task set and the exact intention; more often than not body shapes should be extreme, not 'in between'. Whereas in the past good posture was concerned mainly with sitting and standing and good style was restricted in large measure to how prescribed gymnastic movements were performed, children should learn that good style is important to all positions and activities.

As with many other themes, teachers might prefer to teach two or three consecutive lessons on this theme and then to return to it subsequently as appropriate and necessary.

Apparatus
The shape of the body is often determined by the outline of the apparatus and the spaces presented by its arrangement. Ropes, bars and window ladders offer many points of support and provide many opportunities for the body to be inverted with security, which cannot be so easily experienced on other portable apparatus. Changing the shape of the body while travelling can also be experienced on this apparatus.

Opening activities
1 Dead men in threes. (One person stands completely stiff and falls backwards to be slowed down and stopped by the outstretched arms of one of his partners who then pushes him back to the vertical and on to the outstretched arms of the third person and so on.)
2 Balance or walk on hands.
3 Run and split-leap from one foot to the other.

4

5

Floorwork
1 Stand in a really good balance position on one foot, then sink and roll away to an excellent sitting position. Repeat using other starting and finishing positions and rolls.
2 a) Walk b) trot c) hop d) jump e) roll f) move in crab position g) bunny hop h) cartwheel i) spin j) lunge from one position to another, concentrating on very clear shapes and good style.

3 Travel freely but slowly on both feet, passing *through* various physically demanding contrasting and very stylish body shapes.
4 Construct and perfect a short sequence selecting components from 2 above.
5 Select four extremely good contrasting body shapes, two while on the left foot and two on the right foot. Perfect a suitable sequence involving travel *through* those shapes.
6 Travel freely but slowly and deliberately. Transfer weight from and on to various combinations of body parts but concentrate on moving stylishly at all times.
7 Isolate several components from 6 above and put them into a really good sequence.
8 Select four contrasting balances, some of them upside down, and join them together into a stylish non-stop sequence.
9 Run and jump and try to take up two contrasting shapes in mid-air before landing.
10 Take up a very good shape on the floor and then run and jump to take up the same shape in mid-air. Repeat with other shapes.
11 Balance on one foot in an extremely good but difficult body shape. Remain balancing on the same foot but gradually change to other body shapes. Continue on the other foot.
12 Take up a long bridge shape on hands and feet. Gradually move individual body parts to change the body shape in pleasing stylish ways.
13 Transfer body weight from feet to hands to feet and so on, concentrating all the time on producing clear good shapes.
14 Take weight on one or two parts and show a very good shape. Find several other good shapes, keeping weight on the same part or parts.
15 Roll around the hall freely but deliberately concentrating on taking up excellent and contrasting body shapes.
16 Find many ways of arching the body sideways, forwards and backwards while producing excellent body shapes. Put several of them into a pleasing non-stop sequence.
17 Perfect a short sequence which shows a contrast of curled and stretched shapes.
18 Travel five metres moving through several contrasting twisted and straight shapes.
19 Find and practise several movements in which you travel one or two metres in the same position all the time.

20

21

Apparatus
1 Move on the apparatus and surrounding floor in a deliberate way, concentrating on passing through very good contrasting body shapes.
2 Perfect a short sequence on the apparatus and floor which shows a contrast between different very good held positions. Join them with continuous fluent movement.
3 Move about the apparatus with the body sometimes upside down, concentrating on passing through very wide or very narrow body shapes.

4 Move on the apparatus and floor, concentrating on linking the four basic body shapes with twists, turns, rolls and jumps. (Long, wide, rounded, twisted.)

5 Travel through the air on to and off the apparatus to show varied body shapes. (Low apparatus will encourage children to jump upwards rather than to 'drop' down.)

6

7

Closing activities

1 Pairs. Help each other in a difficult balance.

2 Run and jump to touch feet with hands in mid-air in several different ways.

3 Cartwheels.

4

5

Support themes

1 Directions

2 Partner work – coaching

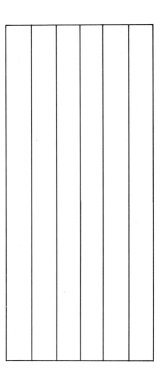

Much depends on the exact intention of the gymnast

Partner work

matching and mirror movements

It is easier to perform simultaneous matching movements when both partners face the same way and one works behind the other. In this way, one person can be the instigator and his partner can see him easily. This type of work was covered in Theme 33.

Matching work performed with partners side by side is obviously more difficult because usually each has to look at the other out of the corner of his eye. Additionally, it is much more difficult for one to be the instigator or leader.

The first part (A) of this theme involves partners working side by side. The second part (B) involves partners facing each other with one person reacting as if he were the mirror image of his partner. Here when one person moves to his left, the partner moves to his right, when one person raises his right hand and looks at it, the partner does likewise, but to his left hand. If one moves backwards, the partner moves backwards using the same movements and timing.

There are several ways in which work on this theme can be approached. One person can move, slowly at first, and his partner has to react immediately. This can be great fun

and it can also be very difficult and therefore rewarding when carried out successfully. In another approach, one person can demonstrate a sequence before both perform it matching each other. In another approach, both discuss and then produce a joint venture. This brings the best results but should not be the only approach used because of that.

Apparatus
This work can become very difficult on apparatus unless it is very simple, low and stable. It is better to have one small piece of apparatus between two, than expect six or eight to work together on a large complicated piece of apparatus. Obviously, gymnasts cannot achieve identical work unless the apparatus both partners work on is identical.

It is essential that children co-operate with each other and never compete against each other. Children must be told never to attempt work which they are not sure they or their partner can manage safely.

Opening activities
1 Pairs. Follow-my-leader with a two metre gap using only named activities like running, jumping, bunny hops, cartwheels, etc.
2 Trot three paces and jump to land in different balance positions.
3 Move freely, sometimes slowly and sometimes very quickly.

4

5

Floorwork
A
1 Stand two metres apart side by side, facing the same direction and in identical starting positions. *Without* prior consultation one slowly stretches and curls sideways, upwards and downwards and partner matches his movements.
2 Perform as in 1, but *with* prior consultation and joint planning, practise a short sequence.
3 Start one and a half metres apart, side by side and facing the same direction. One demonstrates a simple sequence from a stretch balance on one leg and rolls *forwards* into a different stretch balance on one leg. He repeats this sequence and then both perform this sequence simultaneously and identically.
4 Perform as in 3 but simple sequences of own choice.
5 Perform as in 3, but simple sequences of own choice, moving *backwards*.
6 Perform as in 3, but simple sequences of own choice, moving sidewards left and right.

7 Stand side by side one and a half metres apart. One demonstrates a sequence of movements following an angular or curving pathway which returns him to his starting position. Both then perform it simultaneously and identically.

B
8 Face each other with hands touching the 'mirror'. Slowly move one, later both, hands a) in a circular (polishing) action b) towards and away from the 'mirror'.
9 Face each other two metres apart with 'mirror' in between. One slowly curls and stretches and partner reflects.
10 As in 9, but in a variety of other starting positions, e.g. on shoulders and elbows, on all fours, *sideways on* to the 'mirror'.
11 Face each other five metres each side of a 'mirror'. Perform short sequences containing movement towards, at and away from the 'mirror'.
12 Face each other two metres each side of a 'mirror'. Practise sequences moving sideways along the mirror and back again.
13 Face each other five metres each side of a 'mirror'. Practise sequences following circular, square and triangular pathways.

14

15

Apparatus
A
1 Pairs. Get on to the apparatus side by side in an identical way. Visit various parts of the apparatus and take up many identical positions while side by side. Leave the apparatus side by side and identically.
2 Practise simple sequences side by side involving approaching, crossing and moving away from the apparatus.

B
3 Stand on the apparatus facing each other. Plan a short sequence of mirror curls and stretches in various directions.
4 Stand facing each other on the floor at opposite sides or ends of the apparatus. Travel forwards to held positions close to each other on the apparatus and then move backwards to the original starting position.

5

6

Closing activities
1 Balance on hands in many different ways.
2 Mix high and low jumps with rolls.
3 Pairs. One balances on his partner.

4

5

Support themes
1 Symmetrical and asymmetrical movements
2 Quickly and slowly

Theme 43

Time

acceleration and deceleration

Theme 28 was concerned with the performance of movements either very quickly or very slowly. Children learned that some actions, by their very nature, demand to be performed slowly, some need to be performed quickly, and some can be performed either slowly or quickly but probably have an optimum speed. They learned that much depends on the exact intention of the performer and, to a more limited degree, on his or her physique and also that 'quick' and 'slow' are comparative not definitive terms.

This theme is concerned with how this speed or slowness is attained, i.e. it is concerned with acceleration and deceleration. Depending on the activity concerned it is possible for speed to be achieved either explosively or gradually and, again depending on the activity, it is possible to slow and stop in a very short space of time or over a long period. If the intention is purely functional and, for example, one wishes to make a very long leap the climax of a sequence, the period of acceleration must be concerned solely with getting the performer without waste of energy to the right take-off position with good poise at the best (not necessarily maximum) speed.

In many cases, especially in apparatus work, the climax is concerned with vigorous and speedy activity and occurs at about three-quarters of the way through the movement or sequence. However, there is no need for this always to be the case; children can accelerate to a climax, then slow down before accelerating to another climax, and so on. Likewise, they can make the climax a slow sustained movement or even a balance. In this way controlled deceleration would precede the main climax of the sequence.

Additionally, it should be remembered that while gymnastics is mainly functional, it also has an aesthetic quality; constructive use of acceleration and deceleration can make a movement look and feel good as well as being efficient.

Opening activities
1 Run and jump with tucks, stretches and turns.
2 Move continuously taking weight on various parts.
3 Pairs. Find various ways of carrying each other safely.

4

5

Floorwork
1 Run freely, alternating between bursts of high speed and sudden stops.
2 Run freely, alternating between steady acceleration to high speed and steady deceleration to stop.
3 Perform as in 1 and 2 but use methods of travelling other than running, e.g. consecutive jumps, use of hands and feet, rolling, from feet to hands to feet.
4 Run anticlockwise, taking five seconds to attain very high speed and five seconds deceleration to stop. Repeat several times and then change to other proportions, e.g. seven and three seconds, three and seven seconds, etc.
5 Perform as in 4 but use methods of travel other than running.
6 Construct several short pleasing sequences, concentrating on a) a steady acceleration to a climax and a sudden deceleration to a final held position b) a sudden acceleration to a climax and a lengthy deceleration to a final held position.
7 Practise and perfect sequences containing several sudden climaxes joined by movements performed at a steady speed.
8 Practise and perfect sequences involving jumps, rolls, balances and twists showing gentle accelerations and decelerations.

9 Run and jump, first for height and then for length, before landing and stopping. Experiment to find the best speed of acceleration and length of run up for each type of jump.
10 Run and jump, making a very clear shape in the air. Find several interesting ways of decelerating to a stop or landing to stop in a balance.
11 Pairs. Stand side by side. Travel eight paces in unison, accelerating gradually, and then take off one foot, jump in the air and land in a good balance position. Repeat for good quality work and timing. Later practise the same sequence but starting apart and working towards each other.
12 Pairs. Start facing each other ten metres apart. Travel at a steady speed towards each other and stop a metre apart. Perform an explosive action away from each other and decelerate gradually to a good finishing position. Try to keep in time with each other.
13 Pairs. Compose and practise several sequences performed simultaneously involving **a**) a lengthy build-up to a fast climax and a sudden stop **b**) an explosive acceleration to a climax and a slow deceleration to stop. Use various methods of travelling.

14

15

Apparatus
1 **Move** at varying speeds and without prior planning on the apparatus and surrounding floor.
2 Find ways of using the apparatus and the surrounding floor in which steady acceleration can be the main feature.
3 Find several ways of accelerating towards the apparatus, moving slowly along or across it and accelerating away from it to a sudden stop.
4 Find several ways of accelerating towards the apparatus and travelling over it quickly before slowing down to stop on the floor.

5

6

Closing activities
1 Pairs. Travel around the hall twisting and turning in and out of each other.
2 Pairs. Assist each other in difficult balances.
3 Try to walk or balance on hands.

4

5

Support themes
1 Pathways
2 Symmetry and asymmetry

Apparatus work
more advanced

Previous work has been concerned with travelling mainly by means of step-like actions, or by actions which involve flight or by rolling or by spinning when the body remains in contact with the ground.

Sliding is another way of travelling and can be most exciting and enjoyable. Weight is not normally transferred from one part of the body to another part and the body remains in contact with the floor or apparatus.

Sliding in a hall must obviously be done on splinter-free surfaces which can be sloping or horizontal, close to the floor or high above it. Sliding need not be practised in isolation but can be used as an interesting and contrasting part of a sequence. It also serves as invaluable initial experience for such very popular activities as sliding on ice, roller and ice skating, skate boarding, water and snow skiing.

Sliding would be much more easily accomplished were the gymnast allowed to slide on stockinged feet, in a track suit or on a special pad of some slippery material. (The author has not yet experimented in this way.)

Apparatus, in contrast to the floor, can be gripped. Therefore travelling can result from gripping with one part then gripping with another part and releasing the first grip. The body can be above, below or to the side of the apparatus.

Children, young and old, love to use playground swings; swinging on ropes or swinging on fixed apparatus using just the body requires a fair amount of strength as well as nerve and for both these reasons is a valuable and interesting activity. Few school halls possess ropes and therefore swinging normally takes place as a result of gripping the apparatus with, for example, the hands, elbows, armpits, the back of the knees or the stomach. It is important that children swing gently at first and that, if they intend dropping off the apparatus to land on their feet on the floor, they stop swinging first. A skilled teacher might allow some of the more able children to swing, release their hands and land on the floor, but this must be done under control at the end of a backward swing when their stomach is downwards facing the floor and when the hands can be used to absorb some of their weight in the event of an unbalanced landing. In fact, at the end of the swing, the gymnast pulls on his arms to stop the backward momentum and then gently pushes away from the bar and releases his grip. Injury can easily happen in a poor landing after a forward swing and release and therefore a teacher should stand by and support if this activity is to take place.

Swinging sideways can be very enjoyable and swinging can lead into travelling.

Opening activities
1 Practise a favourite movement.
2 Devise a sequence which involves extremely fast and very slow movement.
3 Pairs. Devise and practise a mirror sequence involving moving towards and away from each other.

4

5

Floorwork
1 Lie on your back, front and other parts. Slide around the hall by pushing with hands and feet.
2 Lie on your back with feet against a wall and legs bent. Slide as far as possible by a vigorous pushing off from the wall.
3 Pairs and threes. Find ways in which one person can be helped to slide or spin by his partners.
4 Find various ways of travelling by swinging one or more parts of the body.

5

6

Apparatus

1 Cross the apparatus at different places, working as high above it as possible and safe. Return keeping close to the apparatus.

2 Find many ways of mounting and dismounting different parts of the apparatus by rolling or sliding. Lead the movement with various areas of the body.

3 Visit all parts of the apparatus, travelling when possible either by sliding (pushing, pulling or using gravity) or by rolling.

4 Find which body parts can be used to grip various pieces of the apparatus while remaining above it, to one side or below it.

5 Travel on top of, to one side of, or below the apparatus by gripping, releasing, then gripping with other parts and so on.

6 Travel around the apparatus trying to alternate between being on top of it and below it. Try not to touch the floor unless absolutely necessary.

7 Move skilfully around on the apparatus trying to find where the body can be held in the air between two pieces of apparatus, between the apparatus and the floor or sideways from one piece of apparatus.

8 Find many methods and places where you can jump from the floor preferably to grip and hang from the apparatus; or grip the apparatus and jump the rest of the body on to or over it, or jump to take up a good balance position on the apparatus.

9 Find places on the apparatus to grip with various parts of the body and swing sideways or forwards and backwards. Sometimes use the swing to lead into travelling, but always stop swinging before releasing and dropping to the floor.

10 Travel on the apparatus to find as many places and methods as possible to dismount safely with hands leading.

11 Travel on or suspended from the apparatus, concentrating on having the hips, knees or feet as the highest parts.

12 Move on, under or in and out of pieces of the apparatus using mainly the hands and arms to pull, push or swing the body or to 'walk' on.

13 Travel on the apparatus to find places where the body can spin around a part of the apparatus or on a body part.

14 Produce a good sequence on the floor and apparatus involving rolls, slides, spins, gripping and release, and swinging.

15

16

Closing activities

1 Balance in various ways on hands or forearms.
2 Pairs. Follow-my-leader, travelling mainly by use of hands and feet.
3 Roll, balance, roll, balance and so on.

4

5

Support themes

1 Symmetry and asymmetry
2 Partner work – matching movement

Partner work and work in threes

body management

Previous partner work has been involved mainly with performing similar or contrasting work, negotiating each other without contact, helping each other in simple balances and bearing each other's weight in simple fashion. In this theme gymnasts will be given further experience in some of these activities, but they will concentrate on how they can best support or control safely each other's activities. To do this, they will need to learn the best grips to use when a partner is still, or moving steadily, or moving in a jerky fashion, or maybe turning.

Lifting a partner or helping him into flight will be covered in Themes 47 and 51.

Floorwork
Gymnasts should keep their back straight while pulling or pushing; thighs and buttocks supply the force.

In some activities, partners will have to adopt identical positions, but in many this need not be the case.

Except for 7 and 8 all these activities should take place with a feeling of co-operation, not competition.

Apparatus
It is important that teachers ensure that the apparatus they choose to use is strong enough, stable enough and low enough.

Safety is extremely important and so gymnasts should concentrate on doing simple things well before attempting more difficult activities.

Opening activities
1 Follow-my-leader freely around the hall.
2 Travel freely on zigzagging converging pathways. On meeting, one travels over the other and continues.
3 Face each other and perform interesting mirror activities.

4

5

Floorwork
1 Face each other and use a butcher's grip with both hands to pull firmly but *steadily* against each other. Repeat using one hand only and sideways on.
2 Find several ways of gripping first each other's hands, then each other's hands and wrists, and lastly hands and arms in order to pull against each other firmly but *steadily*.
3 Find various ways of gripping each other's hands, wrists and arms which will resist firm but *jerky* pulls.
4 Face partner and press palms together. Push gradually but firmly against each other. Find other ways of pushing each other using palms against various parts of the body.
5 Find and practise various grips which will allow partners to push against each other firmly but jerkily. (Partners need not be standing and need not use hands only to push or grip. Shoulders, arms, elbows, backs, soles of feet, heads, sides, can all be used.)
6 Find various starting positions and use various body parts to pull and push against each other a) firmly and steadily b) jerkily.
7 Face each other with right wrists gripped and body sideways on. On agreed signal pull very strongly but steadily to move partner. Immediately one person is moved, stop and start again. Invent other pulling competitions.

8 Lean forward and face partner right shoulder to right shoulder and head tucked under partner's chest. Clasp arms around partner's shoulders. Push very strongly and firmly to move partner backwards, stop and start again. Invent other pushing competitions.

9 Practise several good linked positions in which one person balances on the other.

10 Practise several good linked balances in which one person grips his partner in a counter-tension position while at the same time supporting all his weight. (Refer to Theme 37.)

11 Find ways in which one person travels through the air and his partner reaches out to either grasp or push against him to slow him down and lower him to the ground.

12 Threes. Find several positions on feet and on other parts in which each person is out of balance but because each *leans* against the others a combined balance is achieved.

13 Threes. Find several positions on feet and on other parts in which each person is out of balance but because each grips and leans away from the others a combined balance is achieved.

14 Threes. Find several combined balances which can be performed at low level and then raised to high level without losing contact.

15 Threes. Practise various balances in which each person is in balance individually but where all three grip each other so that the resulting balance is pleasing to hold and to watch.

16 Threes. Practise various combined positions in which one person is helping his partners to hold very difficult balances.

17 Threes. Practise several good balances in which two persons' weight is evenly distributed between the floor and the third person.

18

19

Apparatus

1 Use the apparatus and surrounding floor either to take up combined balances or to assist each other to hold a very difficult balance.

2 Take up various combined positions where one person's weight is evenly distributed between the apparatus and his partner or partners.

3 Find ways in which one person travels across, under, along or off the apparatus and his partner helps to support or steady him.

4

5

Closing activities

1 Cartwheel around the hall.

2 Leap and roll.

3 Travel sideways using many interesting modes of travel.

4

5

Flow

The flow factor of a particular activity is to do with the gymnast's ability to stop or change it in mid-stream. At one end of the spectrum is bound flow, when the gymnast has complete control and can stop the activity at will. In the middle of the spectrum, the gymnast moves in a flowing continuous way with no intention of stopping but the ability to do so fairly soon. At the other end of the spectrum, free flow, the gymnast goes full out and cannot stop at any time except when he has planned to do so.

Most gymnastic movement falls somewhere in the middle range; it is done under reasonable control and often has a fluid flowing character. Some gymnastics, probably the most exciting, e.g. flight, is fast and vigorous and has a character not far short of gay abandon. This sort of work should form a substantial part of a class's work as long as the children and the teacher are experienced and the hall large enough.

The confidence, determination and experience of children often affect the sort of work that they produce. However, children should experience as wide a range of free and bound flow movement as possible. They should learn that a sequence can have its character completely changed if its flow factor is altered; they should learn that some activities demand attack and vigour, even if some control is lost, while other activities are best performed in a flowing manner.

It is generally considered that movements should flow smoothly from one to another. Whereas this is normally the case, it is certainly not always so. Jerky movements, swift changes of speed and direction can be very exciting; they can give a sequence vigour and moments of contrast. To take one simple example, jumps could be joined together progressing along a straight line at uniform speed with identical deep and absorbent landings. Alternatively, some landings could be deep, some recoil jerky bounces and some could stop completely.

Apparatus
The choice of apparatus is very important. It is easy to produce flowing continuous work and free work on the level and when going down an incline but not so easy when climbing.

Opening activities
1 Pairs. Join someone you don't normally work with. Follow-my-leader about the hall.
2 Travel about the hall on feet only, sometimes very near to the ground and sometimes high above it.
3 Jump or bounce rhythmically about the hall.

4

5

Floorwork
1 Stand comfortably. Bend, stretch, swing and circle parts of the body so that the movement can be stopped a) immediately at any time b) with difficulty. Repeat from other starting positions.
2 Walk slowly and quickly changing pathways a) jerkily and stopping often b) smoothly and continuously.
3 Walk forwards, backwards and sideways and perform as in 2. Later change the stride length also.
4 Travel in various ways on feet only as in 2.
5 Roll in various directions and speeds a) stopping frequently, sometimes halfway through an action b) smoothly and continuously.
6 Join four bridges and four rolls. Proceed as in 5.
7 Join four jumps together a) stopping frequently b) continuously.
8 Perform a short sequence of runs, jumps and rolls. Proceed as in 7.

9 Take up a balance, jump into another, twist into a third and roll into a fourth **a**) stopping at each balance **b**) continuously and smoothly.
10 Perform a good fifteen second sequence **a**) stopping frequently **b**) continuously and smoothly.
11 Pairs. Plan and perform a sequence along parallel paths **a**) stopping frequently **b**) smoothly and continuously.
12 Travel from feet to hands to feet **a**) under complete control **b**) with attack and verve.

13

14

Apparatus
1 Find many different ways of getting on and off the apparatus **a**) very smoothly **b**) jerkily and stopping.
2 Select a low piece of apparatus and stand facing it about a metre away. Travel across it in several ways using only hands or hands and feet to finish a metre away from it **a**) under complete control **b**) with increasing speed and attack.
3 Take up a good starting position. Move towards, on to, along, off and away from the apparatus to a finishing position **a**) with several stops **b**) smoothly and continuously. Repeat and improve before changing to another sequence.
4 Move on and about the apparatus changing every ten seconds or so from flowing sequences of movement to jerky ones.

5

6

Closing activities
1 Pairs. Help partner to hold a difficult balance.
2 Pairs. One demonstrates a short sequence and partner copies.
3 Try to balance on hands.

4

5

Support themes
1 Personal space
2 Pathways

Theme 47

Partner work

lifting, carrying, pulling and pushing

Lifting, carrying, lowering, pulling and pushing are everyday activities; shopping, luggage, furniture, ladders, televisions, lawnmowers, boats, children, the ill in bed never seem to be where we want them and, what is more, they seem to get heavier year by year. Because so few people know or use the correct techniques, these activities are the cause of a fantastic number of back injuries. For example, up to one-third of all accidents at work arise from lifting and handling tasks.

The techniques of lifting, lowering, pulling and pushing are quite simple and very specific; they do not alter appreciably according to the person's build, age or strength. Consequently, it is essential that these techniques are taught and coached before anyone attempts to move any moderately heavy objects or persons. Having learned and become competent in the techniques involved using imaginary or lightweight objects, children can begin to experiment to find the best ways of lifting heavier and more cumbersome articles or people. This stage of experiment is important because, when the children grow up, they will have to move wardrobes, tea chests, etc., and no two situations will be alike, although the principles will be the same. It is most important, however, that the teacher insists that all children use safe and efficient techniques. They should also learn to combine with others to lift heavy or cumbersome objects; a weight shared is a weight halved.

Good lifting, pulling and pushing techniques recognise that although the back might be willing it is very weak, especially when bent or being used at an angle to the line of action. It should not be used as a source of power, only to transmit the power required. This means that it must be kept as straight as possible and pointing in the direction of pull, push or lift.

All lifting, pulling and pushing should be done by straightening the legs, thereby using the strong muscles of the thighs and buttocks. The shoulders and arms are also fairly strong and can be used reasonably safely. If this technique were always taught properly, it should mean that mothers would no longer lift their babies by keeping their legs straight and bending their backs.

Lifting
The first rule of lifting is to think before acting. If the weight cannot be lifted with confidence, it should not be lifted at all. Instead, help should be sought. If the children are confident they can lift an object, they should first get close to it. Their feet should be placed a comfortable distance apart facing the way they want to move. The weight should be evenly distributed between the feet, possibly with one foot slightly in front of the other if this means that the object to be carried can be brought closer to the body. If it is impossible to point their feet in the correct direction and they have to turn to move off, they should pivot on the balls of the feet. They should get down to the level of the load by bending the hips and knees. Kneeling on one knee should be avoided; this is a common but dangerous practice. The back should be kept straight from head to tail, with chin in; it should not be twisted, bent to one side or rotated. The upturned hands, crook of the elbows or shoulders should be placed underneath the object, and the object kept close to the body when the legs are straightened.

It is easier to lift an object from a platform (about 60 cm high) than from the ground.

Pushing
Often the best way to push an object is to lean backwards against it and push with the hips straightening the legs. In this way the spine is not used. If this is not possible, the children should face the object and lean against it with the shoulders low and the back straight. They should then push via the hands or shoulders by straightening the legs.

Pulling
If the object is heavy, the children should go round the other side and push backwards with their backsides. If this is impossible, they should grasp the object and lean backwards with shoulders low and back straight and pull by straightening the legs.

Opening activities
1 Jump about the hall, concentrating on vigorous actions of the arms and chest.
2 Try to walk on hands.
3 Travel about the hall from feet to hands to feet and so on.

4

5

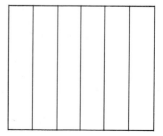

Floorwork

A Lifting

1 **a**) Explain and demonstrate the correct lifting techniques.
b) Practise lifting imaginary objects from hip height and from floor level.

2 Lift, carry and lower light pieces of low apparatus and equipment or lift and lower one end of a heavier piece.

3 Pairs. (Gymnasts should be reminded of how to lift objects from ground level.) Work together lifting and carrying and lowering various pieces of low and light pieces of apparatus or equipment.

4 Pairs. Find interesting ways in which A takes up a low position on the floor and B lifts part of him off the ground.

5 Groups of three. Find interesting ways in which two can lift the third person to a position in mid-air, the combined body pattern being distinctive and pleasing. Hold for a few seconds and lower person safely to the ground **a**) while stationary **b**) while moving.

6 Pairs. A lifts various pieces and types of apparatus or equipment and passes them to B who receives and lowers to the ground.

7 Pairs. Lift various pieces of equipment (or a third person) and place them on top of a higher piece of apparatus. Return them to a space on the floor and continue with other pieces of equipment.

8 Pairs. A stands with legs partially bent and one in front of the other; B climbs on his back under control; A straightens legs and carries B three or four metres before stopping and lowering him.

9 Pairs. Discuss and practise several activities in which A takes up a variety of starting positions with feet firmly on the ground and legs bent. He makes a back or other platform for B who gets on in one of various positions. A lifts B by straightening his legs and then lowers him.

10 Pairs. Practise various combined movements in which A takes up various simple standing positions and B, using correct techniques, lifts, carries and lowers him, e.g. fireman's lift.

11 Pairs. **a**) A stands with legs bent and head high. B stands behind with hands on the shoulders of A. Both time their actions to lift B to a high balance position on A. **b**) Discuss and practise other combined movements in which both work to lift one into a high balance position on the other.

12 Pairs. Find several ways in which A grips B so that when B gets up and travels he transports A.

13 Threes. Discuss and practise various ways in which two lift the third and then lower him safely on to a part or parts other than the feet.

B Pushing

14 (The teacher should explain and demonstrate the correct way to push an object **a**) with stomach towards the ground **b**) with stomach towards the ceiling.) Take up correct pushing positions against a wall and push firmly against it.

15 Pairs. Balance against each other back to back with arms linked and with legs forward and partially bent. On agreed signal try to push partner backwards firmly and continuously. When one is moved a short distance, stop and repeat.

16 Pairs. Scrummage against partner, right shoulder to right shoulder, head under his chest and gripping him with arms and hands. On agreed signal try to push him backwards a short distance firmly and continuously.

C *Pulling*

17 (The teacher should explain and demonstrate correct pulling techniques.) Pairs. Grasp each end of a rope or each other's wrists, lean backwards with legs partially bent and on an agreed signal pull firmly against each other **a)** co-operating to practise the technique **b)** competitively to try to pull partner a short distance.

18

19

Closing activities
1 Travel backwards around the hall on various parts of the body.
2 Travel in various ways but very slowly.
3 Travel in various ways either very close to the ground or far from it.

4

5

Support theme
The many lifting, carrying, pushing and pulling competitions which can be used when the pupils are skilled at the techniques.

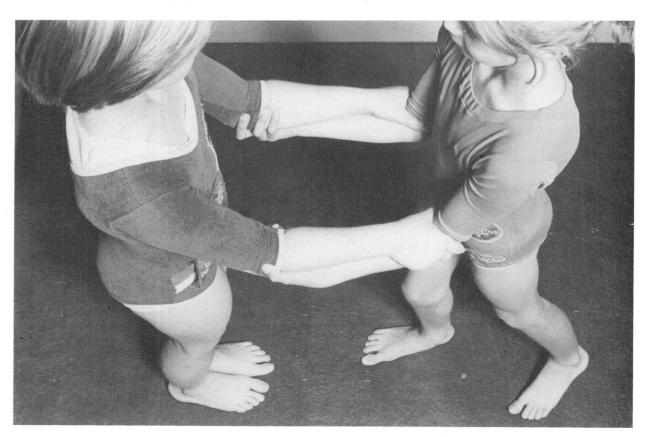

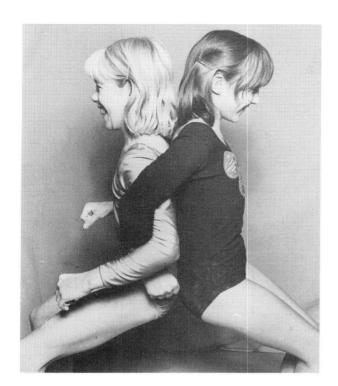
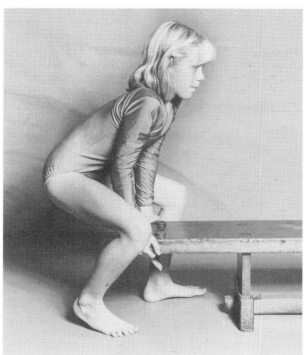
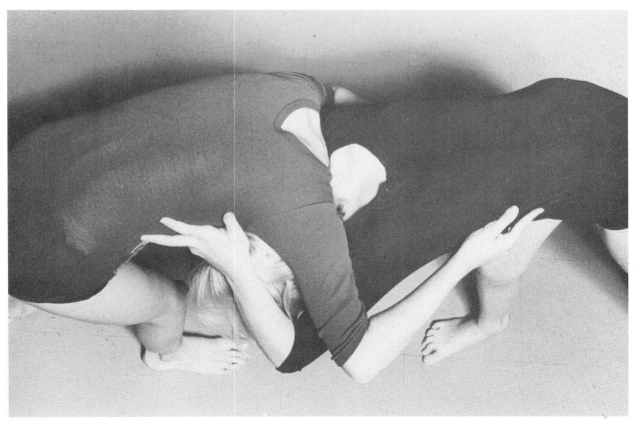

Sequences

more advanced and more planning ahead

The teaching notes on Themes 27 and 36 concerned with sequences will remind teachers and children of what has already been said and discovered. There might also be some parts of these themes which were not taught through lack of time.

Despite the emphasis being placed on the composition of movement sequences, it must be said that there is a definite need in gymnastics for isolated gymnastic actions. Teachers might wish to include some during this theme in order to retain a balance, but none have been included in the writing on this theme.

By this time the gymnasts will be very experienced, and probably very able. With their background they will be able to produce very good spontaneous sequences and will have had much experience of this while practising the skills of other themes. The emphasis in this theme should be on thoroughly planning sequences in advance of their performance. The sequences will need to be refined, or in a few cases, substantially altered. This process should not be hurried and the teacher should be willing to advise and coach or to have the class working in pairs so that they can observe and assist each other to polish their sequences.

When the work has been completed, and the teaching notes of Theme 36 have been gone through, gymnasts should ask themselves how well their sequence answers the task set by the teacher, whether the climax (climaxes) of the sequence is clear and in the best place, and how original and fresh the sequence is.

Taught successfully, this theme will further help gymnasts to plan ahead the best answer to a task, to analyse a sequence, to imagine the feeling within their body of the activities they intend to perform, to remember the action they have performed, to be critical of their actions, and to improve their movement memory. This experience could be applied to other sports. It is known, for example, that it pays swimmers and athletes to spend some time before their event thinking themselves through their activity.

Opening activities
1 Travel about the hall using step-like movements.
2 Travel about the hall frequently taking weight on hands and with legs as high as possible.
3 Pairs. Leapfrog about the hall.

4

5

Floorwork
1 Plan and carry out two very good sequences performed on the spot and including flight, the body sometimes being inverted and taking up different shapes. (Moving on the spot has not featured much in previous themes. Some gymnasts might run on the spot, move rhythmically, sway, twist on the spot from bridge shape to bridge shape, etc.)
2 Experiment to find two very good sequences in which the body sometimes travels, sometimes moves on the spot and sometimes is still. (See note to 1.)
3 Plan and perform good sequences in which the hands move high into the air, then on to or near the ground and then the feet move high into the air and then on or near the ground.
4 Find several good sequences and polish one to perfection in which the body moves sometimes very close to the floor and sometimes far away from it.
5 Perfect four good sequences, the first showing contrasts of speed, the second of direction, the third of flow and the fourth of pathway.

6 Plan a good sequence which involves holding several different balances, sometimes moving out of them by overbalancing under control on to other parts, sometimes placing other parts on to the ground and moving on to them, and sometimes flying from one set of body parts to others.

7 Discover ways in which various parts of the body can be swung through the air and be brought down to the ground safely and under control. Plan and practise sequences involving travelling a few metres and various parts of the body swinging. (Limbs and body parts can be swung horizontally and obliquely as well as up and down. Various body parts can lead the movement.)

8 Practise several sequences in which the top part of the body moves, curls and stretches, takes up shapes etc., in a similar fashion to the lower part of the body (This might well be something that gymnasts have not considered before and therefore they will need plenty of time for experimenting.)

9 Practise several sequences involving sometimes twisting in and out of different balance positions and sometimes overbalancing from one position into the next.

10 Plan and practise sequences in which the arms are used to initiate a) jumps b) turns c) spins d) cartwheel-type actions.

11 Plan a sequence in which a leg is used to initiate a) flight b) turns c) twists d) cartwheel-type actions.

12 Perform a spontaneous sequence in which various inverted balances are joined by different rolls of differing speeds.

13 First work spontaneously and later plan and practise a sequence which involves travelling along the sides of an imaginary square on the ground, moving differently along each side and holding a balance at each corner.

14 First work spontaneously and later plan and practise a sequence which includes four different turning jumps.

15 Pairs. Plan and practise a sequence where both move towards each other, one supports his partner in a balance or supports his weight or catches him in mid-air before both disengage and move away to finishing positions.

16 Pairs. Prepare a good sequence lasting about thirty seconds in which both cross over, under and on each other.

17

18

Apparatus

1 Use ropes individually or in pairs and construct a short sequence using them in various ways for skipping, swinging and moving over when placed on the ground. (The putting down and picking up of the rope should also be part of the sequence.)

2 Travel between and on to two pieces of apparatus and construct a sequence which includes among other activities a spring or dive on to hands and a cartwheel-type action.

3 Practise a sequence in which the body weight is frequently taken on or by the hands and arms, sometimes straight, sometimes bent and sometimes one straight and the other bent. (Sometimes on top of, sometimes levered sideways from, and sometimes hanging from the apparatus.)

4 Prepare a varied sequence on the apparatus and surrounding floor which involves flight, stillness, slow and quick activity in any order.

5

6

Closing activities
1 Pairs. One leads the other about the hall, travelling by different methods. Partner copies whenever it is safe to do so.
2 Travel about the hall in various ways slowly, under control and stealthily.
3 Roll, balance, roll, balance about the hall.

4

5

Support themes
1 Symmetry and asymmetry
2 Pathways

Theme 49

Rhythm and timing

Rhythm plays a very large part in our lives both consciously and unconsciously and, taught sensitively, children love to work using rhythm. Rhythm is treated here as patterns, probably repeated, of strong and weak actions; of activity and stillness; of increase and decrease; of curling and stretching; of pathways that body parts follow, etc.

Rhythm is used in dance probably more than in gymnastics and it could be said, with some justification, that some of the work outlined here would fall as readily, if not more readily, into a dance lesson. Labels and compartmentalising are not all that important, especially with children, and this theme, as well as several others, can be used as a bridge between gymnastics and dance.

Most children can appreciate rhythm quite easily when clapped out, and physically when their feet come in contact with the ground, as in astride jumping. Nevertheless most actions have rhythm, often concerned with the tension which exists in the muscles at different times; the repeated movement of the elbow pressing backwards is an easy activity in which children can feel such rhythm, but much finer delicate movements can be used with more experienced movers. Additionally, people have their own natural rhythm which probably depends in large measure on their age, size, strength and maybe sex.

Competent and experienced gymnasts can move rhythmically on apparatus, but young inexperienced gymnasts find it difficult. Young children can use a single, simple piece of apparatus in this way as long as the activity or sequence of actions is short and simple. If several pieces of apparatus have to be joined together, each gymnast should restrict himself to a certain part of it.

Opening activities
1 Pairs. Leapfrog.
2 Run and jump to perform scissors high jumps. Sometimes take off the left foot and sometimes the right.
3 Take up a good balance position. Overbalance under control into a roll to a good finishing position. Continue with other balances and rolls.

4

5

Floorwork
1 The teacher claps out a rhythmical pattern and keeps repeating it. The children join in as soon as they can. The teacher changes to clap another pattern.
2 Lie on backs and raise, then lower heels, astride, together, astride, together to touch the ground in time with the teacher's gradually changing hand clap.
3 Walk in and out of each other in time to the steady hand clap of the teacher. The teacher gradually quickens or slows clapping.
4 Perform as in 3 above, but instead of walking, run, jump, skip step, giant step, etc.
5 Pairs. Walk rhythmically and in time with each other, one setting the pace. Gradually change the speed and the pathway. Change leadership. (The rhythm need not be completely regular (as with heart beats) but could be slow, slow, slow, slow, quick, quick, quick, quick.)
6 Perform as in 4 above but in lines of four instead of pairs.

7 Skip around the hall being aware of rhythm. Stop and clap quietly the rhythm of your skipping. Continue but, instead of skipping, hop, jump, slip step sideways, etc.

8 Pairs. Trot around the hall to come to a commonly agreed rhythm. Take it in turn to lead and travel around the hall using a variety of foot-only ways of moving.

9 Jump the feet astride, together, astride, together and so on to the teacher's clapping. Work together in pairs to find other interesting and rhythmical jumping movements **a**) on the spot **b**) moving.

10 The teacher claps out a simple rhythmical phrase and repeats it several times. The children experiment to find a good way of moving on feet only to the rhythm **a**) on the spot **b**) while moving.

11 Compose and practise a short sequence involving travel on feet only to your own rhythmical pattern which accelerates and decelerates. (Children can be asked to click fingers or use their voice, or clap out the rhythm at the same time as they are performing the action.)

12 **a**) Stand astride facing the teacher with arms sideways. Arms circling and later elbows circling to the teacher's voice **b**) Work individually to find a variety of repeated rhythmical movements of arms, e.g. elbow pressing backwards, arm pressing backwards, arm swinging, touching toes and standing up, etc. **c**) Pairs. Combine to prepare and practise a sequence of various arm actions to various rhythms.

13 Experiment to find several simple rhythmical sequences involving movements of the arms and legs either at the same time or one after the other **a**) on the spot **b**) travelling.

14 Pairs. One performs a rhythmical sequence lasting about fifteen seconds and composed of interesting curls and stretches. Partner observes and claps out or speaks the rhythm. Repeat with sequences involving **a**) various rolls **b**) various twists **c**) a run, jump and landing.

15 Pairs. One demonstrates twice a simple rhythmical sequence lasting about fifteen seconds and then partner copies the sequence and the rhythm **a**) jumping only **b**) several different rolls **c**) travelling on hands and feet **d**) travelling through several curled and stretched positions.

16 Pairs. Compose and practise a rhythmical identical sequence starting ten metres apart, travelling towards each other, passing and parting to a finishing position.

17 Prepare a ten second sequence in which the climax, a jump, is towards the end. Alter the sequence slightly so that the climax is in a different place.

18 Prepare a fairly long sequence in which there are two climaxes. (It is interesting sometimes to see if observers can tell where the performer intends the climaxes to be.)

19 Pairs. **a**) One person astride jumps rhythmically with elbows bent. Partner stands behind and supports him under the elbows. By increasing and decreasing the lift given on successive jumps he slows down or quickens the jumper's rhythm. **b**) Find other ways in which one person's rhythmical movement can be altered with the help of a partner. (The performer need not be standing.)

20

21

Apparatus

A *With skipping ropes*

1 Find a space. Skip on the spot with the rope turning **a)** forwards **b)** backwards, concentrating on the various rhythms that can be used.
2 Perform as in 1 but travelling.
3 Use the rope and a variety of skipping actions and swings of the rope to produce interesting rhythms.
4 Pairs. With one rope either held by one or both, perform as in 3 above.

B *With other apparatus*

5 Find a single piece of apparatus on which to develop an action which can be repeated rhythmically. Use the same piece of apparatus and find another answer to the task before moving to another piece of apparatus. (Children could, for example, circle around a horizontal bar; swing on a rope; jump over a piece of apparatus; mount and dismount apparatus in various ways; roll backwards and forwards on a box, bench, mat, etc; hang by arms or legs and swing; raise and lower body by heaving and stretching; etc.)
6 Develop a short rhythmical sequence on the floor and apparatus.

7

8

Closing activities

1 Mix different high and low jumps with rolls into a pleasing sequence.
2 Travel in several ways on hands only.
3 Pairs. Travel over or under each other, sometimes with contact and sometimes without.

4

5

Theme 50

Partner work

directions and pathways, meeting and passing, mirror movements

Floorwork A

The pair work should be performed as follows: one person demonstrates his actions or sequence, his partner observes it, and then copies it, and finally, where possible, both perform the sequence in unison.

It should be remembered that pathways are either direct or indirect; that the gymnast can travel forwards, sideways, backwards, head first or feet first, etc., while following a given pathway; that a gymnast can change direction part-way through his sequence and that there are several methods of so doing.

In order to remind pupils of the work they have done previously on pathways and directions it will probably be best if they work individually before they work with a partner.

Floorwork B

Partners have previously negotiated each other, helped each other to balance, supported each other's weight, shared apparatus and space, as well as copied each other's pathways, movements and sequences.

This theme is designed to help them plan and practise ways in which they can approach each other, pass and leave each other during combined sequence work. They have done this to a limited extent during matching sequences and so the emphasis here should be on compatible sequences but not necessarily matching work. The pathways they follow can show immense variety as can the ways in which they pass each other.

Floorwork C

Mirror movements performed with backs to the mirror are obviously much more difficult than those performed facing the mirror. However, they can be made easier if both turn their heads sideways for they have a chance of being able to see each other out of the corner of their eyes.

Opening activities

1 Run about the hall performing tucked, straight and piked jumps. (A piked jump is one in which the body is bent at the waist and the fingers touch the toes.)
2 Travel about the hall, sometimes using vigorous explosive movements and sometimes slow and deliberate movements.
3 Travel about the hall with sometimes the toes and sometimes the fingers as the highest point.

4

5

Floorwork

A *Directions and pathways*

1 Travel individually in exciting ways, but concentrating on following a variety of indirect pathways while always facing the direction of travel.
2 Travel as in 1 above but sometimes travel forwards, sometimes sideways and sometimes backwards.
3 Pairs. One faces a destination ten metres away and travels to it using various foot-only methods. Partner observes and copies.
4 Pairs. One travels as in 3 but changes part way through the journey to travelling sideways and then to travelling backwards. Partner observes and copies.
5 Pairs. One travels on various parts of the body in a straight line to a destination ten metres away. Partner observes and copies.

6 Pairs. One travels on various parts of the body in a straight line to a destination ten metres away but changes his direction of travel part way through his journey. Partner observes and copies. (The teacher could stipulate that they travel using flight, rolls, stepping, twisting, turning, etc.)

7 Pairs. One travels using various foot-only methods to a destination ten metres away *following a flexible pathway* but facing forwards all the time. Partner observes and copies.

8 Pairs. Perform as in 7 but sometimes travelling forwards, sometimes sideways and sometimes backwards.

9 Pairs. One travels on various parts of the body along a flexible pathway with a change of direction mid-way through the journey to a destination ten metres away. Partner observes and copies. (The teacher could stipulate that they travel using flight, rolls, stepping, twisting, turning, etc.)

10 Pairs. One travels on various parts of the body away from and back to his starting place following **a)** a circular **b)** an eliptical **c)** a rectangular **d)** a free-choice pathway while at the same time introducing one change of direction. Partner observes and copies.

B *Meeting and passing*

11 Pairs. Start opposite each other ten metres apart. Move towards each other, pass and part to finish where your partner started. (Partners can travel under, over, through or to the side of each other. They can support each other, help each other to balance or take up a combined position. The teacher might have to remind them that they should not always travel in a forward direction.)

12 Pairs. Decide on a flexible pathway and, starting from opposite ends of it, approach, meet and part to finish where your partner started.

13 Pairs. Compose and practise sequences which involve interesting methods of travel, changes of direction and also pathways in which partners meet and pass each other several times. (Both can use different methods of travelling; pathways can converge and part at various angles and levels or can move along parallel tracks.)

C *Mirror movements – backs to the mirror*

14 Pairs. One adopts a simple balance position with his back to an imaginary mirror. Partner stands to one side to observe, then moves to the correct place 'behind' the mirror and adopts an image of his partner's balance position. Continue with other simple curled, twisted and stretched shapes, facing away from the mirror. (The teacher might have to remind the class of what mirror work is by having them work on the spot *facing* a mirror first.)

15 Pairs. Plan and practise several simple mirror movements which can be performed in unison on the spot with backs to the mirror between them. (Sufficient time for discussion and planning must be given.)

16 Pairs. Plan and practise a simple sequence in which both start with their backs to the imaginary mirror between them and travel away from it to a destination five metres away **a)** on feet only **b)** using other methods of travel. (Pupils should be reminded that it is better to perform a simple sequence well than a complicated one badly. However, if they become capable in this work, a change of pathway and direction could be suggested.)

119

Apparatus

1 Pairs. One approaches, travels over, along or across his apparatus, and leaves it to travel to a destination away from it. He concentrates on good but simple methods of travel and follows an interesting pathway, sometimes travelling forwards, sideways and backwards. Partner observes and copies.
2 Pairs. Plan and practise a sequence in which partners approach and pass each other several times on the apparatus, each time differently.
3 Pairs. Plan and practise a sequence of mirror moves on or suspended from the apparatus **a**) on the spot **b**) while travelling, in which both have their backs to the imaginary mirror between them.

4

5

Closing activities

1 Take up a good bridge shape on hands and feet and then push up on to fingers and toes. Repeat with other bridge shapes on combinations of hands and/or feet.
2 Take long slow steps about the hall, taking weight on toes, then pivoting on them before lowering the heel and stepping away again.
3 Roll sideways about the hall, sometimes tucked up and sometimes straight.

4

5

Support themes

1 Moving rhythmically
2 Body shape

Flight

more advanced and partner-assisted

Flight is concerned with travelling through the air without support and by now children will be particularly adept at one of its forms, jumping. Flight can take place in upward, sideways, forward and downward directions, can be performed on to, over, along and off apparatus or other people, and gymnasts can be assisted into flight. Many parts of the body can be used for take-off and landing and the gymnast can somersault, twist, turn, curl, stretch, etc., in mid-air. With able gymnasts, the emphasis should normally be on height obtained in flight because this is the factor above all which gives gymnasts time in the air to perform exciting activities.

Partners can be used to good advantage, not only to produce flight but also to control it. They can lift each other, throw each other, act as a platform for each other and project each other with their legs, etc. They can alter the rhythm of jumps, speed up or slow down spins, support each other in a difficult jump, catch each other and help each other to land under control.

Apparatus can also open up opportunities for flight, not only because of the extra height it affords and therefore the extra time in the air that it gives, but also because it allows gymnasts to swing off it, spin off it and fly off it sideways or downwards using body parts not normally strong enough to produce flight in an upward direction.

Apparatus
Only apparatus which is strong, stable and will not slide should be used. In some cases, the edge of the stage can be used, but in any case make sure that there is plenty of low apparatus with mats (surrounding it if possible). This will allow the children to experiment with their flight in relative safety and to find many ways in which to land. A low piece of apparatus placed beside a high piece of apparatus also opens up possibilities.

Opening activities
1 Run and jump for height. On landing, reach out for the ground with stretched legs in order to gradually control the body weight.
2 Jump **a**) sideways **b**) backwards, concentrating on good landings.
3 Jump and spin in mid-air at various speeds, concentrating on good landings.
4 Trot and jump for length. Land with **a**) both feet level **b**) one foot in front **c**) on both feet and then take one step forward to control the speed.
5 Practise a variety of scissor jumps and good landings.

6

7

Floorwork
A *More advanced*
1 Run and jump with various shapes, twists and spins in mid-air to land on a small mark on the floor.
2 Jump variously to take up shapes which involve the whole body in **a**) symmetrical **b**) asymmetrical **c**) wide **d**) fore and aft **e**) tucked positions. (The children should use all their body to produce a shape, and should be warned not to rotate in a forward or backward direction when tucked.)
3 Take up two different shapes in mid-air during a single jump.
4 Discover as many parts as possible which can project the body into the air. (Mats should be used. Children will learn that some parts cannot easily produce much height.)

5 Bounce on as many different parts of the body as possible. (Mats should be used.)

6 Discover which parts of the body can be used for landing from various sorts of flight. (Mats should be used.)

7 Find several ways of causing flight mainly by swinging a leg or both legs. Use other parts of the body to swing you into flight. (Many different starting positions can be used.)

8 Travel through the air, taking off and landing on various parts of the body. Perform a sequence of three or four different sorts of flight a) facing forwards along a straight line b) facing different ways along a straight line c) facing different ways along a flexible pathway. (Mats should be used. Several combinations of parts can be used for take-off, e.g. one hand and one foot, two feet and one hand, hands and head, hands and shoulders, shins.)

9 Find various ways of taking off the feet, travelling through the air to land on hands. Gradually increase the height or length of flight. (Some children might try various cartwheel-type actions.)

10 Find different ways of flying through the air and landing in a difficult balance position.

11 Jump in various ways, leaning slightly forwards on take-off. In the first jumps regain an upright position before landing and in the later jumps land while still leaning forwards. Repeat but leaning slightly sideways on take off. (To regain the vertical position in flight is an extremely valuable safety factor. Children sometimes fall off apparatus or walls, etc., and if they are able, in good time, to push off in the correct direction with their feet, they will be able to land safely.)

12 Jump to land on one foot with the trunk leaning forwards and nearly horizontal. Repeat with other jumps and turns in the air.

B *Partner-assisted*

13 Pairs. Both stand and find ways in which one helps the other to fly higher, or further or differently. (The class should be reminded of safe lifting techniques (Theme 47). They could lift each other under elbows, grasping wrists, facing each other, one behind the other, etc.)

14 Pairs. Grip wrists, link elbows or similar parts to find several ways in which both are active but one helps to throw the other into the air while retaining contact with him. Landings must be safe. (At first, children should retain contact with each other and gradually increase the strength they use in order to throw each other.)

15 Pairs. One sits and both find ways in which he can help his partner to travel through the air.

16 Pairs. One lies on his back with feet bent above him and partly supporting his partner. He gently straightens his legs to project his partner into the air to a safe landing. Find similar ways of projecting each other. (This is for sensible children only. Mats should always be used.)

17 Pairs. Find ways in which one helps the other to travel backwards through the air to land safely.

18 Pairs. Find several ways in which one travels through the air and the other supports him towards the end of the flight and assists him to land safely.

19 Pairs. Find several ways in which one can help the other to spin safely a) on the floor b) in mid-air.

Small-group work

Most children love to work together in small groups and, given sufficient time and judicious help, will produce an excellent variety and standard of combined gymnastics. This theme extends further the physical and social skills required in working together harmoniously, and it goes without saying that only children who are well versed in pair work and also well behaved and motivated should be introduced to this work.

It is important that sufficient time be given for gymnasts to discuss, plan and then perfect their work before finding another response to the task set.

It will be found in most cases that one opening activity, one floorwork task, one apparatus task and one closing activity will be all that can be covered in a lesson.

Apparatus
At least in the first lessons on this theme, the apparatus should be simple (i.e. not many pieces are combined into one grouping), stable and fairly low.

Opening activities
1 Practise various tucked and straight jumps, all turning in mid-air. (Gymnasts should be required to go through very good positions in mid-air.)
2 Balance on hands in various ways for several seconds.
3 Move continuously about the hall in various ways but sometimes slowly and sometimes quickly.

4

5

Floorwork
A *Threes*
1 Find several ways in which to work together as a group a) while stationary b) while travelling.
2 Find several ways in which two can grasp the third person, lift him into the air for several seconds before lowering him safely to the ground a) while stationary b) while travelling. (Children should be reminded of good lifting techniques – Theme 47.)
3 Find several ways in which two can grasp the third and swing him before lowering him safely to the ground.
4 Find several ways in which two can help the third to fly through the air and to land safely either with or without support.
5 Discuss, plan and practise several group actions in which one travels through the air and then is caught, supported or controlled by the other two in such a way that he lands safely.
6 Invent and improve upon several actions in which each gymnast is either in counter-balance or counter-tension. (Counter-balances are those which involve leaning inwards and counter-tensions those which involve leaning outwards (Theme 37). Starting positions need not be on feet.)
7 Follow-my-leader activities about the hall in which the pathway is copied exactly and the activities as nearly as can be done safely.

8 Discuss and perfect several short sequences in which all perform the same activities in exactly the same way at the same time. (If necessary, gymnasts should be reminded that this can be done side by side, behind each other or facing each other.)

9 Plan and perform several sequences in which all three converge on one spot, and take up a combined balance before moving away to a finishing position.

10 Invent continuous patterns of movement which involve members of the group jumping over each other and then rolling. (Each group will require at least one mat.)

11 Invent several short sequences of movement which involve the members of the group working in canon. (Working in canon is when first one person moves, closely followed by the next and then the next, e.g. A tips over into a balance on hands and feet followed immediately by B, then C; A jumps legs through hands followed by B, then C; A rolls sideways followed by B, then C, etc.)

12 Practise several sequences in which members of the group travel across the hall following a converging and then diverging pathway.

B *Fours*

13 Find several ways in which to work together as a group **a)** while stationary **b)** while travelling.

14 Find several group actions which involve at least one of the members working first at low level then at high level and lastly at low level again.

15

16

Apparatus (threes)

1 Plan and practise several sequences involving each gymnast starting at a different place on the floor and travelling towards the apparatus, then moving along, across or under it, and lastly travelling on the floor away from it.

2 Find several sequences which include **a)** two helping the third person to hold a difficult balance on the apparatus **b)** a group counter-balance or counter-tension held on the apparatus.

3 Find and practise several ways in which two help the third person to **a)** travel off the apparatus in a difficult way but safely **b)** travel across or along the apparatus in a difficult way but safely.

4

5

Closing activities

1 Balance on hands with legs high. Lower legs to the ground under control, sometimes to the left and sometimes to the right of hands.

2 Roll about the hall in various directions, sometimes curled and sometimes stretched.

3 Run, jump, land and roll about the hall.

4

5